Write with Me:

Partnering with Parents in Writing Instruction

Lynda Wade Sentz

EYE ON EDUCATION
6 DEPOT WAY WEST, SUITE 106
LARCHMONT, NY 10538
(914) 833–0551
(914) 833–0761 fax
www.eyeoneducation.com

A sincere effort has been made to supply the identity of those who have created specific strategies. Any omissions have been unintentional.

For information about permission to reproduce selections from this book, write: Eye On Education, Permissions Dept., Suite 106, 6 Depot Way West, Larchmont, NY 10538.

Library of Congress Cataloging-in-Publication Data

Sentz, Lynda Wade.
  Write with me : partnering with parents in writing instruction / by Lynda Wade Sentz.
     p. cm.
  Includes bibliographical references.
  ISBN 978-1-59667-163-8
  1. English language—Composition and exercises—Study and teaching. 2. Education—Parent participation. I. Title.
  LB1576.S343418 2010
  372.62'3--dc22

                                                                    2010027610

10 9 8 7 6 5 4 3 2 1

Also Available from EYE ON EDUCATION

Family Reading Night
Darcy Hutchins, Marsha Greenfeld, and Joyce Epstein

Building A Culture of Literacy Month-by-Month
Hilarie Davis

Active Literacy Across the Curriculum
Heidi Hayes Jacobs

Teaching Grammar: What *Really* Works
Amy Benjamin and Joan Berger

**Motivating Every Student in Literacy
(Including the Highly Unmotivated!) Grades 3-6**
Sandra K. Athans and Denise Ashe Devine

**Literacy from A to Z: Engaging Students in
Reading, Writing, Speaking and Listening**
Barbara R. Blackburn

**Classroom Motivation from A to Z: How to
Engage Your Students in Learning**
Barbara R. Blackburn

**Teach My Kid, I Dare You! The Educator's
Essential Guide to Parent Involvement**
Sherrel Bergmann, Judith Brough, and David Shepard

**Dealing With Difficult Parents
(And With Parents in Difficult Situations)**
Todd Whitaker and Douglas J. Fiore

Family Math Night: Math Standards in Action
Jennifer Taylor-Cox

101 Poems for Teachers
Annette Breaux, Illustrated by L. Susan Brandt

Seven Simple Secrets: What the Best Teachers Know and Do
Annette Breaux and Todd Whitaker

What Great Teachers Do *Differently*: 14 Things that Matter Most
Todd Whitaker

Dedicated to…

my parents, Patty Wade Simpson and the late
Donald Wade, who raised me to love words;

my husband, Jonathan, without whose love, support,
and encouragement this book would have not been written;

my children, Tim, Tyler, Taylor, and Thomas, who showed me the
power of sharing writing between parent and child.

Acknowledgements

Special thanks to the original mother–son journaling team, Christine and Nathan Roach. You inspired my research in the realm of family journaling, and it is because of the writing you did together, that I began to study the parents and children writing together. Were it not for a conversation about a parent–child journal years ago, there would be no book on the topic of parents as writing role models today.

Many thanks to the administration and Board of Education of Frontier Central School District in Hamburg, New York, for providing me with the resources and opportunities to grow as a writing teacher. Each day that I spend in my classroom, I am given the opportunity to continue building a community of writers. Additionally, I must acknowledge my colleagues at Cloverbank Elementary School. Many thanks for your kind words, support, and above all, your commitment to making writing a priority.

To my students and the writing families at Cloverbank Elementary School, I thank you for helping inspire a new generation of writers. You have shared, generously, your heartfelt words in your journals so that others may read your words and be moved to action. Writing will take its rightful place in education because of those who care enough to write.

Free Downloads

The following figures are helpful for launching the parent–child partner journal and writing scrapbook, and they are available in full size on Eye On Education's website. Permission has been granted to purchasers of this book to download and print these figures. You can access these downloads by visiting Eye On Education's website: www.eyeoneducation.com. Click on the **Free** section, or search or browse our website to find this book's page.

You'll need your bookbuyer access code: **WWM-7163-8**

Bonus: Additional samples of parent–child journal entries are also available online. They illustrate writing from students in a variety of primary grade levels and include the author's notes and observations.

Contents

Meet the Author

Lynda Wade Sentz graduated from State University College at Buffalo with a Bachelor of Science degree in Elementary Education and English Education. She received her Master of Science in English Education from State University College at Buffalo and holds New York State Teacher Certification in both Childhood Education and Secondary English Education. She is currently a classroom teacher at Cloverbank Elementary School, Frontier Central School District in Hamburg, New York, which lies just outside the city of Buffalo. Lynda has taught in both public school and parochial school settings in general education, resource classroom and inclusion classroom settings.

Lynda has authored numerous children's stories, poems, and a large volume of newspaper articles and editorial pieces. Her work has appeared in *Buffalo News*, *Rochester Democrat and Chronicle*, *Children's Playmate Magazine*, *Hopscotch Magazine*, *Boys Quest Magazine*, Bee Group Newspapers, *Hamburg Sun*, *Western New York Family Magazine*, and *Medical Community Digest*, to name a few. In addition, her fiction work has been acquired by Florida State Education Department for use in the F-CAT assessment administered in Florida schools.

Lynda is married and is the mother of four sons, who all learned at a tender age to craft their words with care.

Introduction

Here's the secret of writing: there is no secret.
— Ralph Fletcher, author

"I hate to write."

Did you ever speak those words? Did you ever think those words? These are among the most dangerous of all words because they reflect an attitude that can and will damage young people. Just as we pass language and culture on to our children, we also hand down our values and our attitudes toward education. Particularly with writing, negative feelings are evident when one avoids writing tasks. This negative mindset can get passed down from one generation to the next and can prevent future generations from learning to love the craft of writing.

I've encountered three kinds of parents. The first type are parents who seem to intrinsically understand the educational needs of their child, regardless of whether they have any educational training or not. They just know exactly what to do to build their child up and increase the academic strength of the child. Whether it is reading with their child, taking them on educational outings or writing with their child, they just *know* what to do.

The second type are parents who may not take it upon themselves to try new things or come up with new ways to increase their child's academic skills. These are the parents, however, who will do *anything* a teacher asks in the belief they are helping their child. In that spirit, if you ask them to drill multiplication facts, they are on top of it. If you ask them to read with the child, they do it. If you suggest they write with their child, they will take up the pen and write.

Less often, I've met the third type of parent, the parent who resists becoming involved in the educational process. When it comes to writing, this can be problematic. I once encountered a parent who would not write with her child even though the child wanted desperately to have her mother write with her in her partner journal. The mother refused the child week after week, then finally called me and gave me quite a tongue-lashing. After assuring me that she did not have five minutes a week to spend writing with her child, she let me know that furthermore, she hated to write and wasn't good at it. Now, no one enjoys getting yelled at by a parent, but that isn't what hurt me that day.

What does hurt is when parents express those negative feelings about writing so strongly, because I know what their child is missing—a vital role model. The child who has no parent to share writing with misses the richness of the bond that forms between the two writers, the indescribable bond that comes with shared words. That hurts me, but the real damage is done to the child, particularly if the negative feelings about writing are transferred to the child. That is damage that may be irreversible.

I firmly believe that the mom referenced earlier could easily manage to carve out five minutes for her child. Although she spent much time trying to convince me that she had no time to write with her child, neither of us really were buying it. When she got to the part about not being good at writing, we were at the heart of the matter. She felt incompetent as a writer because of bad experiences in school with writing. From those bad experiences, she became fearful, and that fear was the impediment to her willingness to write with her own child.

Words, shared between two souls, are a gift. Writing is a glimpse inside the heart of another. There is nothing more personal than reading the written words of a loved one in a note or letter. There is nothing more personally risky than putting your own writing out there for others to read, reflect, and criticize. One thing I have learned as I teach writing to students is that there is no better way to get to know a student on a completely different level than by reading the child's writing. Regardless of the topic and the format, the voice of the child is there, waiting to be listened to. For a parent not to take advantage of that opportunity makes me very sad. For a parent to be so scarred by their writing experiences in school, makes it even sadder.

My quest is to educate parents and offer them that gift to share with their child. Without the parent as a writing role model, there will forever be a gap in a student's writing education, no matter what writing curriculum a school chooses to use, no matter what we as educators do. Just as a teacher can never be a replacement for the parent, a teacher can never fill the gap in a student's education if they don't have a parent for a writing role model.

As a result of the research that has been done over the decades in the area of writing, and because of my own experiences as a writer, I encourage parents to increase their participation in writing activities, particularly with their children. I urge colleagues to try and create their own mentor text pieces and share those pieces with their students. I know the difference it will make for students when writing is evident around them and becomes a part of the fabric of their life.

It is truly not enough for a student to have the occasional teacher who loves to write. It is not enough for a student to see their parent scratch out a quick note or a card every now and again. Writing needs to assume a place of great importance in the classroom and, particularly, outside the classroom, in the home.

Purpose
(a.k.a. How to Use
This Book)

At its best, writing has helped transform the world. Revolutions have been started by it. Oppression has been toppled by it. American life has become richer because people like Rachel Carson, Cesar Chavez, Thomas Jefferson, and Martin Luther King Jr. have given voice to the aspirations of the nation and its people. And it has become fuller because writers…have explored the range of human misery and joy. When pressed, many of us, young and old alike, still turn to pen and ink in the effort to make sense of our grief, pleasure, rage, or happiness.

— National Commission on Writing,
"The Neglected R" (2003)

Let's face it. We have our students for about six hours each day. The remaining hours can either reinforce what we teach or completely undo all our hard work. I wrote this book to inspire teachers across the nation to lift writing up, to elevate it to a place of importance in the classroom and in the home. Regardless of how you teach writing in your classroom, you need to get the parents involved to seal the deal for students. Your students absolutely need to see their parents rally to the cause of creating powerful writing and writing for enjoyment.

Writing success for students isn't about working harder. It isn't about creating better units, handing out more worksheets, coming up with better writing prompts or even finding a new curriculum or a different methodology. It isn't about creating cuter, more eye-catching displays of writing. It is about engaging the parents and encouraging them to model writing in the home. Parents are perhaps the most underutilized resource in education, yet they are the most powerful tool in the teacher's arsenal.

Reality Check

Parents have all the clues as to what makes their children tick. Although teachers spend the month of September trying to get to know students, the parents already know everything about them. Likewise, while students are sitting in their seats that first day wondering about us, the person standing in front of them in the classroom, they already know what to expect from mom and dad. By pulling parents into the mix, garnering their support for classroom activities, particularly when it comes to matters of literacy, the teachers strengthen their position as educator. Parents can support the learning that takes places in the classroom or completely undo the work that has been done.

In 2006, the National Commission on Writing (NCW) issued *Writing and School Reform*, a report that calls for an in-depth look at each and every school, how writing instruction is carried out in each school, and the need for creating a writing climate, a writing community, if you will, inside every school. The report reiterated the need for effective practices in the classroom, and found that although there is much great work happening in schools, more needs to be done. The need for continued professional development exists as well as the need to personalize instruction for students. The report urged Americans to continue forward on a path toward continued writing achievement.

Educators and experts encourage parents to read to their children, but parents rarely get the message that they should write with them as well. Research also shows, however, that although we do not make the same push for parents to write with their children, Americans do view writing as important and think the need exists to place more emphasis on writing. A study published in November 2005 by the National Writing Project (NWP) states that more than 72 percent of Americans strongly agree that a person needs to be able to write well to advance in almost any career or job, which seems like common sense. In addition, Americans believe that all future teachers should receive advanced training in the teaching of writing, and that such training should be put into practice now. In other words, those Americans in the workplace now realize (perhaps) their own shortcomings in writing ability and also realize that they did not learn everything in school that they needed to learn.

Parents want more for their children. Ultimately, the goal for educators should be to educate in a way that causes our young people to become proficient communicators so that they can compete in the global workplace. As we have seen a push for proficiency in math and science, educators are now pushing for proficiency in writing. Writing skills are coming to the forefront in the job market. Employers want to hire competent writers.

Roots and Wings

In purely practical terms, writing is at the very root of our way of life and popular culture, often in subtle ways. Although it is clear that every book, magazine and novel is the work of a writer, we forget that every movie, commercial, theatrical production, instruction manual, and even cereal box exists because someone wrote the text it contains. Although only a few hundred thousand adults earn their living as full-time writers, many Americans would not be able to hold their jobs if they were not excellent writers. The number of full-time writers is expected to grow at a faster pace in the coming years.

Writing, then, is far more important than improving scores on standardized tests, acquiring a job, advancing a career, or producing the next pop culture icon. It is about being a citizen, understanding the world around you and preserving our way of life and our freedom. It is about encouraging others to do the same. Writing gives the power to change the world. The future success of our society depends upon the reflective, thoughtful work of educated individuals who read and write with competence and passion.

As children learn to write, they learn to think. The process of writing one's thoughts carries with it the process of thinking in organized ways. In other words, much of what is put on paper has been created and synthesized internally first. The mental processes thus engaged strengthen those abilities required to process information in other areas of education and as a lifelong learner. Therefore, writing should not only be given importance across the curriculum but also in the hours when school is not in session.

This book is not another writing program. The information contained herein is designed to be used in conjunction with, as a supplement to, the writing program already in place. It is not about teaching according to a different process or using a new program. It is about changing attitudes about composing. It is all about utilizing the best tool we have at our disposal—parents. It's about giving our children roots—a firm grounding in writing. From roots, our children grow wings.

The key factors to building parent support for writing are attitude, interest, ease, and enjoyment.

Attitude

Beginning in September, it is imperative to build a relationship with your families and set the tone for a wonderful year of writing right from the start. This book contains a plan for making parents their child's writing partner starting with that first contact, ending when you send students off for the summer. Approaching the writing year with positive, warm expectations that include parent participation set the stage for student success. Building enthusiasm for writing while maintaining a nonthreatening set of expectations is a year-long balancing act.

The enthusiasm of the teacher for the craft of writing is a critical component of a writing plan. This is not always an easy hurdle to overcome for teachers. If the teacher loves to write, this part has been mastered. If the teacher feels less confident as a writer, the teacher will need to get more comfortable as a writer. Think about it. If, as a trained professional, one is wary when it comes to writing, how might a parent feel? First things, first. Jump the hurdle; learn to love the craft. A teacher must never ask a parent (or a student) to do something they themselves are not willing to do.

Interest

When given a choice, parents will always participate in activities that interest them. Although writing may not initially be their cup of tea, it is just a hop and a skip to catching their interest. Most people tend to enjoy talking about themselves; writing is just a little hop from talking. It's talking on paper. In essence, the prompts in the journal ask parents to write about memories from their own lives or thoughts and feelings. They also can choose to write about their own topic. The personal nature of what they write makes the writing more like a conversation with their child.

The Partner Journal resources are a starting point for writing teams. Writing is always a journey, and the writer can never be sure where the journey will end. Be ready for writing partners to need additional resources or more direction. Be ready for writing teams to flourish and take off on other projects of their choosing. Every writing partnership is unique. That is the beauty of writing instruction. Not knowing the outcome can also be the most difficult part of the process.

Ease

Busy families face more challenges today than ever before. Although that is true, busy schedules are not sufficient reason to allow parents to be sideline spectators regarding the education of their children. In fact, it is more reason for them to get involved. Every minute counts now like never before. Every assignment teachers send home must maximize learning. There is no time in the curriculum for fluff. There is not a minute to waste. As teachers, we need all the support we can get. Parents are an amazing resource, and the very least we can do is make their job—helping us—as easy as possible.

The Partner Journal is simple and easy. It requires just a very few minutes of writing, and a few more for sharing the writing together. What happens over time is that the partners see each other as real writers and relate to each other in that way. A task doesn't have to be difficult to bring about change. With journaling, the change takes place over time. Students practice what they have learned, and they might even teach the writing partner a thing or two.

Enjoyment

All the activities suggested in this book are intended to make writing seem like a treat rather than a task. Teachers want every writer to look to the challenge of composing words with eagerness, not trepidation. Students pick up on nonverbal cues that tell them how their teacher truly feels about writing. Actions show it. Attitude shines through. When the teacher, the role-model-in-chief, exudes passion for the craft, it will rub off on the students. They will love to write when it becomes fun. Writing for real purposes adds to the excitement. Of course, it goes without saying that writing is never used to punish (e.g., "Write 100 times 'I will not chew gum in school'") students or to correct behavior unrelated to writing instruction.

When considering our parent writers, the same is true. The teacher needs parents of students to look to the task of writing with their child like a bonding experience, like a leisure activity in an otherwise grueling week. Writing time is relaxation time, a chance to regroup and refresh. To that end, the teacher must talk up the writing and offer fun opportunities for family writing. It is necessary to put forth the effort to offer as many options for parents to become writing role models in the home. There are many, many other ways to increase family writing time and enjoyment. The success of family writing rests on the willingness of all parties to consider possibilities.

At first, especially when the concept of family writing is introduced for the very first time, there may be a number of parents who find this business of writing with their children peculiar. Family writing is not often a component of classroom instruction. Reluctant parents can be encouraged, cajoled, and eventually persuaded to join the fun. As one mom put it, "I've talked to other parents. None of them have done this before. We've never heard of anything like this before." Truly. New ground is being broken here, going where few parents have gone before—into a notebook with their children.

Before starting the Partner Journals and the concept of family writing, it is necessary to spend a good amount of time planning for its implementation. It is no small task to put into practice these activities and materials, although it does not have to be difficult. It requires thoroughness and careful consideration, identifying any possible hurdles you may encounter. Tweak and adapt materials as you go. One-size-fits-all does not necessarily apply to writing instruction. The resources may be used as they are or they can be modified as needed—in part or in totality—whatever best serves the needs of teacher, student, and parent.

Finally, if you are using this book for a professional-growth-and-development initiative, book study, critical friends group, literature study group, or a peer collaborative project, there are questions to prompt further thinking and discussion among your group. Additionally, there are questions for reflective purposes after implementation of the Partner Journals. These questions can be revisited at the end of each partner writing cycle or the end of the school year.

1

Parents, Their First Writing Teachers

Writing is for stories to be read, books to be published, poems to be recited, plays to be acted, songs to be sung, newspapers to be shared, letters to be mailed, jokes to be told, notes to be passed, recipes to be cooked, messages to be exchanged, memos to be circulated, announcements to be posted, bills to be collected, posters to be displayed, and diaries to be concealed. Writing is for ideas, action, reflection, and experience. It is not for having your ignorance exposed, your sensitivity destroyed, or your ability assessed.

— Frank Smith, author of
Writing and the Writer

When I think back to childhood, I remember the importance of writing in daily life, especially letters. Long distance telephone calls were perceived to be expensive, but postage was reasonably priced. Letters were the mainstay of the relationship between my mother and grandmother since my mother married and moved away from her rural childhood home. My grandmother, who had a sparse education, wrote letters that kept my mother in touch with her hometown and her relatives. Writing and receiving those letters became as much a life-sustaining resource as water from the pump.

Reading my grandmother's letters, her voice is clear. I can hear her voice as clearly as if I were sitting in her kitchen. I also hear her voice as a writer, and I remember her words and the sound of her speaking voice. The grammar isn't perfect; I always noticed that as a kid reading those letters. But it was my gram, right there on paper. How precious are those lines, scratched out between the minutes when loaves of homemade bread were rising and during the baking.

I'll start you a few lines, don't really have much to write about, mostly about the weather. This is the worst spell we have had for a long time, there is so much snow. And then it froze underneath and new snow on top…it's hard to walk.

There must be at least 12 inches and there is supposed to be more and maybe some freezing rain…about five weeks since we even been to the mailbox and there hasn't been church for five weeks.

If it was on level it would be different, but these hills. Preston County is the place where they have really had it. Some drifts were as high as 25 feet. Patty, this isn't very much to write, but maybe I can think of more next time.

Love to you all,

Mother

It may not have seemed like much to write about according to my grandmother, but that letter was a treasure that my mother kept for all these years that have passed since it was penned in the mid 1980s. My grandmother's West Virginia drawl is in my head as I read her words. I can see her country kitchen and smell the bread cooling on the counter. A little note scribbled in the upper corner of the page, "it was 6 below yesterday morning."

Another thing I do remember is my grandmother's calendar. She would jot down the weather of a particular date and maybe a few other details on the calendar squares. I don't think that she did it every day, but a glance at her calendar revealed a very unique journal. She documented snowfall and when the robins returned to her mountain home. It eventually became a handy almanac to look back at during the next season or the next year. She found it interesting to look back, then compare the current year to the past year, reminisce over whether it was an early spring, late spring, little rain, much rain. Birds and flowers told much about the season. My grandmother documented much of it.

My Role Models

My mother is a list maker. She makes a list for everything. Christmas cookies to make? There's a list. Thanksgiving dinner to prepare? There is most assuredly a list written out detailing what we will eat, easily a month in advance. Creating a list in writing is how she organizes her thoughts and ultimately her actions. The fact that she organizes and thinks this all through in writing is a wonderful life skill that no doubt has helped her streamline her life.

Dad was a serious documenter of all things, a serious record keeper and a detailed travel planner who could write a set of directions from here to wherever in greater detail and with far more accuracy than any online site could manage. My father was also absolutely fanatical about grocery lists. There would never have been a trip to the store sans list. The list was always hanging on the fridge. If anyone in the family emptied a carton of this or a can of that, they were responsible to write the item on the list. During his military days, he was an avid photographer and creator of intricately detailed journaling beside every photo. He was also a letter writer in those days.

The Heart of the Matter

I only recently fully realized all the imperceptible ways my parents were encouraging me to write even from my earliest days. There were always pads of plain white paper, maybe five-by-seven inches in size, in the kitchen junk drawer in my childhood home. I remember cataloguing all my storybooks while pretending to be a librarian.

It is little wonder that in the present day I write copious lists for myself, carefully making a plan for weekend tasks or checklists for days off. Or that I make notes all over my calendars and save them from year to year. They are family artifacts to be treasured, as are family anecdotes and stories scribed in journals. All of these chronicle the life we lived. It is a way of life inherited from my first writing teachers—my mother, my father, and my grandmothers.

In the Garden

Educators sometimes think in terms of plant analogies when discussing the various topics associated with writing. Ideas are seeds. Young, budding writers are tender sprouts in the literary garden that can be nourished and helped to thrive, or allowed to wilt and wither. Because children often begin to write long before they enter the classroom, the young writer is most often first tended to by the parent. The parent, like a gardener, can help the fledgling grow and flourish or allow them to struggle and wilt. A child may have experienced tremendous growth at the tutelage of their writing role model, or they may show only the barest signs of writing knowledge when they arrive in the classroom.

By the time parents have prepared children for formal education, most have devoted substantial time and energy to making sure the child knows vital information such as name, address and phone number by repetition and drilling. Rote memorization, learning something "by heart," allows knowledge to be recalled so quickly that it seems to be woven into the fabric of the child's very essence. Bits of information learned in this way come back instantly, seemingly without requiring a thought.

Unfortunately, the craft of writing is often mistakenly viewed by parents preparing children for school as the ability to form letters and words, with little thought given to the conveyance of ideas. Once the formation of letters and simple words has been accomplished, parents may simply feel they have nothing more to offer the budding writer. They may feel their part in their child's writing education is complete. In order to succeed in the world, though, one must be competent and skilled in the creation of written communication. While the process of writing is not something that can be learned through rote memorization, it is a craft that can be developed so that individuals can compose various types of writing with confidence.

Parents sometimes take a hands-off approach, leaving the bulk of the training in writing to the "experts"—the classroom teachers. Perhaps parents believe schools have all the answers, but the fact is that writing instruction has troubled educators for many years. It has been difficult for educators to agree on the best way to teach others how to write; that debate, which continues today, will likely go on for some time. Although formal writing instruction in the classroom can stimulate and enrich the writing seed the parent has planted, students need every available writing role model they can have access to. Perhaps parents think teachers do not want them involved in this academic area.

Education Is a Lifelong Process

Education is a difficult topic to tackle and impossible to perfect, regardless of the particular aspect of writing being examined. Writing instruction can seem even more unwieldy. What is the ultimate objective of education? Why do we send our children off to a classroom five days a week, six hours a day? Mortimer J. Adler originally stated the case for education in *The Paideia Proposal, An Educational Manifesto* in 1982. According to Adler, the two fundamental goals of formal education are "equipping all the children of this country to earn a good living for themselves" and "to lead good human lives." The greatest need for any student is becoming a literate citizen of the world. A measure of success should be attainable for all. Success in the writing arena cannot guarantee success later in life, but it most certainly will increase the odds of success. Writing instruction impacts every facet of education, every area of life after formal schooling ends.

Although Adler and his followers had many ideas about the form formal education should take, they did not relegate the task of education solely to the "professionals." Adler strongly suggested that traditional schooling is only a small piece of the puzzle. "The simple fact is that educational institutions, even at their best, cannot turn out fully educated men and women. The age at which most human beings attend school prevents that. Youth itself is the most serious impediment—in fact, youth is an insuperable obstacle to being an educated person." That remains true today. The full responsibility for educating successful students who become productive, contributing citizens cannot be laid at the door of the school. There are many hours outside the school day. It is for parents to help a child fill them wisely and make them educationally productive.

How often do students head to college only to change direction within that first year? How often do parents wish they had known much earlier what time has taught them? Adler lays out concrete arguments reflecting his belief that learning neither begins nor ends with formal schooling: "Education is a lifelong process of which schooling is only a small but necessary part." We know that children will continue to learn after they leave us. Children are and should be learning before they arrive at the door of the school. Learning doesn't end at the close of the school day or the school year for that matter. In those unclaimed hours, educational opportunities can take place.

A common misperception about writing pervades our society. Writing is believed to be for scholars and the elite. We elevate the task of writing to such a high level that many adults are reluctant to make the attempt to try writing, much less attempt to teach a skill that is perceived to be so difficult to their children. As discussed by Frank Smith in *Writing and the Writer* (1994), writing is still far too often seen as a difficult task. In spite of the fact that we are no longer dipping quills in ink and writing on parchment, and in spite of abundance and accessibility of electronic devices designed to facilitate human communication, we don't write much as a society.

The notion that writing is too hard, too boring, too whatever, remains. Smith argued that in addition to the actual brain functions required to learn the mechanics of writing, there is something perhaps more difficult to attain. "Learning to write is less an intellectual achievement than a social one, depending on attitude rather than application. Learning to write begins—whatever the writer's age—with seeing oneself as a writer, doing the things writers do, and thinking the way writers think. This is a matter of identity, not of instruction or of effort, even the desire to learn," according to Smith.

Writing can feel like such a solitary activity. After all, one does need a good amount of time and space to compose thoughts. Early on, children are taught to do their own work. We need to see what the child's ability is, and writers must express their own ideas. A reluctant or struggling writer is a sailor adrift in the wide-open sea with no port in sight. Yet, writing is all about communication and sharing one's thoughts and ideas. Young writers need mentors to guide them into port without hindering them from the experiences of the journey.

Parents as Writing Role Models

Attitude and Identity

No matter what a person chooses to do in life, they must see themselves in the role and naturally must have a positive attitude about it. Seems simple enough. See your future and feel good about it. This is how we choose our career paths. We become aware of a particular avocation, wish ourselves into that role, and then set forth on the path to achievement, realizing that it will take some effort on our part to achieve the dream. Writing is no different. We must view writing positively, see ourselves as fully capable of being able to write, then begin trying to become that writer. If we want our children to succeed in life, they must write well. If we want them to write well, they must have a positive attitude toward the craft and see themselves as capable of composing text.

Thomas Steinbeck, the son of legendary author John Steinbeck, is himself an author. Imagine having to live up to the legacy of the man who wrote *The Grapes of Wrath, Of Mice and Men, East of Eden,* and many more great classic pieces of literature from the 20th century. That is a tough act to follow. Yet, it is a great role model to have at home.

"I never saw myself as The Great American Writer, nor did I have any ambition whatsoever to compete with my father, who by the way is one of my literary heroes," the younger Steinbeck said in an interview for *Writers Digest* (2003). "And they're two different people, as far as I'm concerned. There's my father, and then there's John Steinbeck. And you know as much about John Steinbeck as I do. I know a lot more about my father, but those are two different people."

In fact, Thomas Steinbeck shied away from writing as a young adult. Who could blame him? How do you compete with one of the world's truly great writers? You don't. Steinbeck took no interest in writing as a career for quite a long time. "You'd put a pistol to my head, and I wouldn't write," said Steinbeck.

It was when he enlisted in the military and was sent to Vietnam, that the writing bug bit Thomas Steinbeck. During his deployment, he served as a helicopter door gunner, but he began writing about the war as a journalist for a small wire service that his younger brother, John Steinbeck IV, had created. Thomas focused his writing on the human-interest angle of the stories rather than on reporting the news. Perhaps he was channeling his famous author father.

"I was far more concerned with the individual drama of soldiers than I was with the big picture," he said. After his tour of duty, he returned to Vietnam in the late 1960s as a combat photographer.

The love of writing had been instilled in the brothers Steinbeck, although both headed in relatively different directions than their famous father. Nonetheless, the modeling of writing in the home, the love of the written word was passed to the next generation. Today, Thomas Steinbeck has three books to his credit as well as a number of screenplays. He has also written several adaptations of his father's works.

It should come as no surprise that the offspring of writers write. As the children of doctors or lawyers often follow in the footsteps of their parents, so it is with writers. According to researchers at the Cato Institute, there is clearly a link between parental involvement and student achievement. A report issued in 2000, *More Than Grades: How Parent Choice Boosts Parental Involvement and Benefits Children*, stressed parent choice and parent involvement in education as being crucial to student success. According to the report, even though research supports the need for parent involvement and indicates positive impact on achievement, little has been done to effectively increase the amount of parent involvement in schools. The report also contends that parents are an underutilized resource, noting that "even in *Goals 2000*, the first national goals set forth, parent involvement/influence was left out completely." The more things change, the more they stay the same, it seems. We neglect to include the parent component.

Few of us will ever sit down and write a best-selling novel. Very few of us even would want to. But how many of us want to ensure that our students are successful? How many parents want their children to be successful? There are probably few adults, if any, who would not want that, but getting there may feel like an impossible dream. This is the beauty of parents and children journaling together. The cost in terms of time and difficulty can be minimal, but the results are huge and far-reaching. The effects follow our students into every area of their life where they must compose their thoughts or put a pen to the page. Parents can set an example that will last a lifetime through parent-child partner journaling.

Partner journaling can be a quick five-minute activity. No matter how simple the topic, the power of the act of writing together lies in the sharing and the bonding, perhaps more than in the actual words. In this book, journal entries appear one following the other, but when using partner journals, it is recommended that you create the journal in a way that allows the entries to be written on facing pages (Figure 1.1).

Figure 1.1. Partner Journal

Here is a quick father–daughter exchange on paper. The authors of these entries wrote from a generic writing prompt, "Did you ever meet a famous person?" Our children only know about our lives what we show them. A long ago meeting with country singer Willie Nelson might have gone forgotten were it not for this bit of journaling:

"Did You Ever Meet a Famous Person?"

Parent entry:

I did. When I was about 15 years old I was staying with a friend in Elkhart, Indiana (travel trailer capitol of the world). My friend owned a company that made conversion kits for trucks and vans so you could sleep in them. I would go to work with him and do odd jobs around the shop and also did a lot of sweeping up.

One Friday after lunch he called a meeting of all his workers to tell them he had a special job that had to be done over the weekend. He told them that the singer, Willie Nelson's, tour bus had a fire in it and they had just two days to do all the repairs. I got to help, mostly just cleaning up and getting stuff for the real workers. Well, the work got done, not only on time, but early that Sunday, Willie Nelson came to the shop and looked at all the work that had been done and was very happy.

He was so happy that he invited everyone to the hotel restaurant he was staying at for a dinner. I got to sit with my friend and Mr. Nelson. While we ate, he asked me what I wanted to do with my life. I told him I was not sure. He then gave me this advice: Never claim to be the master of any one thing and never stop learning about all things; no matter what you are asked to do, whether it is cleaning a toilet or saving mankind, always do it to the very best of your ability.

It was a good job, a good dinner, and great advice.

Child response:

I think that is *amazing*. The advice was *amazing*. Willie Nelson must be a very nice man.

It is great that you had the chance to meet such a great artist. I'm so glad to have a dad that had the opportunity to do all these things! You actually got to fix the Willie Nelson Tour Bus.

When I grow up, I want to be just like my dad. The way Mr. Nelson talked to you and gave you that advice, it as like he actually knew you as an old friend. I think my dad would give that kind of advice, deep heart-warming tough love advice! It is truly *amazing* what he did, especially since he was only 15.

Even if it was only cleaning, like Willie Nelson says, always do your best!

It seems that as educators, we grasp a piece of the puzzle here and there, yet the whole picture has not quite come into full view. Composition is this ever unwieldy, ever changing, spinning, transforming beast of a subject to wrap the brain around. Depending on your vantage point, it takes on different hues. Little wonder that parents are so widely divided as to their role in the education of their child. Little wonder that educators have had such difficulty in determining the best methodology in teaching composition. Little wonder that we have failed to pinpoint the missing link in writing instruction—parent involvement.

The Survey Says…

In 2006, a group of adults—parents, teachers, and adults with no children—was surveyed about writing in the home. Nearly two-thirds of those who are parents (65%) who responded said that they write for one hour or less each week at home and work combined, leaving only a third who write two or more hours per week. Of that third, 8% say they write for more than four hours each week.

The survey group was drawn from a pool of suburban, middle-income adults with varying levels of education attained, who came from varying socioeconomic states. Additionally, the level of school and community involvement varied among the group. The population of participants represented both single parent and two-parent family situations, and the number of children in each family varied as well; the survey group was purposefully diverse.

The intent of the survey was to determine amount and kinds of writing being done by parents and whether their children have the opportunity to see their parent engaged in the writing process. A secondary focus and added benefit of the survey is making parents more aware of writing in the presence of their child. Participants completed the Parent Writing Inventory that was developed for the purpose of gathering data about parents as writing role models. The Parent Writing Inventory (Figure 1.2, on the facing page) consists of questions geared to help determine whether or not parents model writing behaviors in the home when their children are nearby.

When the survey was first carried out, it was sent by both e-mail and hard copy to parents of school-age children. A number of surveys were forwarded by e-mail by respondents to other friends and colleagues. Some of those respondents had either very young children, no children, or grown children. The data from these individuals, although not originally sought, proved useful in determining whether or not there is a significant difference in responses among those groups. Respondents are parents of children of various ages, ranging from very young children to children who are now grown (Figure 1.3).

Figure 1.3. Parents as Writing Role Models— Demographics and Respondents

Parents	Young Child(ren) Birth to School-age		School-age Children		Older Children (College and Beyond)		Total	
	no.	%	no.	%	no.	%	no.	%
Male	2	5.40	7	18.91	1	2.70	10	27.01
Female	5	13.51	16	43.24	6	16.21	27	72.96
Total	7	18.91	23	62.15	7	18.91	37	99.97

Who Writes?

Survey respondents were both male and female, blue-collar, white-collar, and "no collar," referring to stay-at-home parents (Figure 1.4, page 12). The term *white-collar worker* refers to a salaried professional or an educated worker who performs semiprofessional office, administrative, and sales coordination tasks, as opposed to a blue-collar worker, whose job requires manual labor. "White-collar work" is used as an informal classification, in contrast to "blue-collar work."

Figure 1.2. Parent Survey Questions

Parent Writing Inventory

When you are at home, what kind of writing do you do? How often?

(Check all that apply)	(Circle)				
1. _____ e-mail	daily	weekly	monthly	occasionally	never
2. _____ i-message (instant message)	daily	weekly	monthly	occasionally	never
3. _____ social network	daily	weekly	monthly	occasionally	never
4. _____ text message	daily	weekly	monthly	occasionally	never
5. _____ note	daily	weekly	monthly	occasionally	never
6. _____ letter	daily	weekly	monthly	occasionally	never
7. _____ journal/diary	daily	weekly	monthly	occasionally	never
8. _____ report	daily	weekly	monthly	occasionally	never
9. _____ list	daily	weekly	monthly	occasionally	never

10. Do you ever write newspaper or magazine articles? If so, please give details:

11. Do you ever write short stories? Poems, other pieces of creative writing? If so, please give details:

12. Have you ever written a book or novel?

13. What type of writing do you engage in write when your child is nearby?

14. Do you assist your child(ren) with writing assignments for school? Why or why not?

15. What other types of writing do you compose?

Figure 1.4. Demographics and Socioeconomic Status of All Respondents

Parents	Blue Collar		White Collar		No Collar		Total	
	no.	%	no.	%	no.	%	no.	%
Male	4	8.51	9	19.14	0	-	13	27.65
Female	7	14.89	25	53.19	2	4.25	34	72.33
Total	11	23.40	34	72.33	2	4.25	47	99.98

Survey Question 1: When You Are at Home, What Kind of Writing Do You Do? How Often?

Respondents answered questions about the type of writing they complete in the home (Figure 1.5). Parents stated that lists (91%), e-mails (86%), and notes (86%) are the three types of writing they most often compose, followed by letters (59%), reports (35%), journals (32%), instant messages (27%), and other unspecified types of writing (24%), such as newspaper articles, newsletters, or creative pieces.

Figure 1.5. Type of Writing Parents Complete in the Home (37 Parent Respondents)

Parents of	Shorter Composition				Longer Composition			
	E-mail	IM	List	Note	Letter	Journal	Report	Other
Young Children	7	-	5	4	4	1	–	–
School-age Children	19	8	22	21	15	8	9	8
Older Children, College +	6	2	7	7	3	3	4	1
Total Responses								
Number	32	10	34	32	22	12	13	9
Percent	86.48	27.02	91.89	86.5	59.45	32.43	35.15	24.32

Other = Newspaper, newsletter, creative pieces

It is important to note that at the time of the survey, instant messaging via computer was just becoming extremely popular. Texting via cellular telephones, and messaging through social network sites such as My Space or Facebook, were not yet widely used. Twitter did not yet exist. The virtual explosion of new technology—cellular text messages and social network messaging—increased writing in this way greatly. However, for the purposes of discussing composition, it is important to note that some of the important steps in the writing process—revision and editing—are generally skipped because of the rapidity of communicating in this way. The carryover effect of text language on spelling and grammar in the formal writing makes many educators absolutely shudder.

For the purpose at hand, it is also necessary to state that these forms of communication are not always viewed as "real" writing, as are a number of forms of "writing" listed on the survey. Specifically, list making, and the majority of e-mails that are composed probably do not technically fall into the category of "real" writing either. Where all of these do become important, however, is that parents are modeling the act of "writing," the act of composing, and their children may be nearby. This is good. Additionally, the fact that they are doing these things and enjoying it is also good.

Had the survey been more limited to actual composition—letters, journals, essays, articles, reports, creative forms (short stories, poetry, screenplays), novels, and other books—the results may have revealed a far greater number of nonwriters.

Time After Time

Respondents were also asked to estimate the amount of time they spend writing at home and work combined (Figure 1.6). It is important to note that it is likely that the estimates may be higher than actual amount of time spent writing. Respondents may have intentionally or unintentionally estimated the time somewhat higher than was actually the case. The accuracy is dependent upon the estimation skills of the person surveyed.

Figure 1.6. Number of Hours Parents Spent Writing (Home and Work Combined)

Under 1	1 hour	2 hours	3 hours	More than 4 hours
14	10	5	5	3
37.83%	27.02%	13.51%	13.51%	8.10%

How Much Writing Do Parents Model for Children in the Home Setting?

A major issue this study was to address was how much writing children see their parents composing in the home. The survey results provide data on whether or not parents are modeling writing in the home for their children. The data shows that the amount of writing for enjoyment parents compose increases as the age of their children increases. Perhaps it is a time factor. Older children require less and less parental maintenance as they become more self-sufficient and do more for themselves. Perhaps this frees parents to pursue other interests such as writing. Additionally, parents working in the white-collar sector are slightly more likely to write for enjoyment (38%) than their blue-collar counterparts (22%). Although no participants stated work as a reason why they don't write, it appears to factor into the problem.

Nearly two-thirds of parents (65%) who responded to the survey said that they write for one hour or less each week at home and work combined. That leaves less than a third who write for more than an hour each week. Of that third, only 8% say they write for more than four hours each week. When asked, 13% of respondents stated that they write for two hours per week and another 13% stated they write for three hours each week.

Assuming adults sleep for eight hours a day, there are 112 waking hours in a week. Writing for one hour out of 112 hours amounts to spending less than 1% (.89%) of one's waking hours engaged in writing. However, according to the U.S. Department of Labor, the average adult spends 3.5 hours watching television each day—24.5 total hours for the week and 22% of their waking hours. It seems likely that the average student experiences a parent modeling the art of television watching far more often than the craft of writing.

Again, it is important to remember that the amount of time stated was taken at the word of the survey respondent and could be greater, but it could be much, much less.

Who Writes Because They Like to?

Respondents were queried about writing for enjoyment (Figure 1.7). This yielded a rather interesting piece of information when the survey results were tabulated. This question was an effort to gauge to the extent that adults write for enjoyment and to get parents to consider whether they do or do not actually write because they like to.

**Figure 1.7. Percentage of Parents Who Write
for Enjoyment by Age of Child(ren)**

Write for Enjoy- ment	Young Child(ren) Birth to School-age		School-age Children		Older Children (College +)		Total	
	no.	%	no.	%	no.	%	no.	%
Yes	1	2.70	7	18.91	3	8.10	11	29.72
No	6	16.22	16	43.24	4	10.81	26	70.27
Total	7	18.91	23	62.15	7	18.91	37	99.99

Survey Question 8: Do You Write for Enjoyment?

When asked, 29% of parent respondents stated that they do, indeed, write for enjoyment. However, the overwhelming majority of parent respondents—70%—said that they do not write for enjoyment. One of seven parents of young children (18% of the total survey group) write for enjoyment, whereas seven out of 16 parents of school-age children write for enjoyment. Are we passing our dislike of writing along to our children without meaning to?

Overall, it was found that a greater number of parents say they do not write for enjoyment than the number of parents that do write for enjoyment. Only 29%—less than a third—of those parents queried stated that they do write for enjoyment. Of that group, 18% are parents of school-age children, followed by parents of older children (8%) and finally parents of young children (2%). Parents who do not write for enjoyment (70%) are the vast majority. Almost half are either parents of children currently enrolled in school (43%) or are parents of children who have not enrolled yet (16%).

White-collar parents of school-age children stated they write for enjoyment 38% of the time, slightly better than data for school-age parents in general (Figure 1.8). Data for blue-collar parents finds that only 22% of parents working blue-collar jobs write for enjoyment, compared to 38% of white-collar parents. According to the data, it does make a difference in the likelihood that a parent will be one who writes because they enjoying writing.

Figure 1.8. Percentage of Parents Who Write for Enjoyment by Socioeconomic Background

Socioeco-nomic Back-ground	Young Child(ren) Birth to School-age		School-age Children		Older Children (College-Beyond)		Total	
	yes	no	yes	no	yes	no	yes	no
Blue Collar	–	1	2 22%	7 77%	–	1	2	9
White Collar	1	4	5 38%	8 61%	3	3	9	15
No Collar	–	1	–	1	–	–	–	2
Total								
Number	1	6	7	16	3	4	11	26
Percent	2.70	16.21	18.91	43.23	8.10	10.80	29.71	70.24

Note: All respondents who have no children are white collar
– = no respondents

Here is a sampling of what parents said when they responded to the question, "Do you write for enjoyment?"

♦ "Just this week I have been kicking around the idea of compiling my experiences and reflections on being a parent who just lost a child to leukemia either for therapeutic purposes or potentially to be published."

♦ "I write down descriptions of how I am feeling as a means of sorting through issues."

♦ "No, I am not a very good writer."

♦ "I write letters to family out of town."

♦ "Sometimes—quotes and sayings."

♦ "I write for a variety of purposes in my journal; enjoyment is one purpose. I write creatively within the confines of the required writing at work."

♦ "Nearly all work related, but much of it I enjoy."

♦ "Yes, I try to write daily. Some days are more successful than others. I will typically start journaling. A poem may arise out of something I am feeling in the moment or something I have been pondering. A short story may bubble due to my mood. A need to talk can get me to begin working on the novels. I call this diarrhea of the mouth. I very often will write about research I am doing on a topic of interest and that finds its way into all things during the periods of study."

♦ "Scrapbooks and journaling."

♦ "E-mails and essays daily."

♦ "I maintain a weblog."

♦ "One–two times a week—journal entries, e-mails, and I love writing tutorials to make computers easier to use."

♦ "Not anymore. You don't have kids, do you?"

Writing in the presence of young children can be challenging, but writing can provide an outlet for a stressed parent or one who feels isolated. Writing can provide an opportunity to flex those thinking muscles, a welcome change from the challenges of child rearing duties. Writing can capture those all too fleeting days. Every stage of childhood brings with it a new set of challenges, a new demand on one's time. Small children need more maintenance. School age children need to be driven a great many places. Journaling can be a great activity for a carpooling parent waiting to pick up a gang of kids.

Parents Who Teach

The data collected from respondents who are not parents (Figure 1.9, page 18) and the data collected from parents who are also educators by profession (Figure 1.10, page 18) led to some interesting findings. It was not data that was originally sought, but it provided an interesting frame of reference. It also yielded some stark findings. The data for childless adults is the reverse of the data for parent. Adults who have no children express the opposite sentiment about writing—70% do write for enjoyment, whereas 30% do not write for enjoyment. Perhaps they were raised as writers, or perhaps their time is not divided by the demands of raising children. Whatever the reason, nearly three-quarters of these respondents write for the love of it.

Figure 1.9. Respondents Without Children

Write for Enjoyment	Total	
	number	percent
Yes	7	70
No	3	30
Total	10	100

Figure 1.10. Respondents Who Are Educators (Teachers, Administrators, Professors)

Write for Enjoyment	Total	
	number	percent
Yes	3	27.27
No	8	72.72
Total	11	99.99

Eleven parent respondents to the survey were both parents and educators—classroom teachers, college professors, or administrators. The results for educator parents mirrored the data for parents in general. Eight respondents (72%) do not write for enjoyment whereas only 3 (27%) do write for enjoyment. Although it is easy to assume that educators all certainly must enjoy writing, being an educator by career choice is no guarantee that one will enjoy writing or even be a skilled, confident writer. Writing is a highly personal craft that one learns to enjoy because of modeling by adults in our lives. Not every educator had that example in their life, thus they may not write with their children. Being an educator in no way means we don't fight the same demons with our writing. To the contrary, when it comes to writing, it seems we all fight the same battles whether we teach for a living or not.

Parent respondents were divided into the following categories: parents of young children (18%); parents of school-age children (62%); and parents of older children who are college age or beyond (18%). Of the total parent population surveyed, 27% of respondents were male and 73% were female. Although it was the intent of the study to query an equal number of male and female parents, completed surveys were returned by a grater number of female respondents. When divided by socioeconomic status of respondents, parent respondents were as follows: blue collar, 23%; white collar, 72%; and no collar, 4%.

Lessons Learned

Children learn by the example that is set before them. If books and writing materials are available and are valued, skills associated with literacy will come to the child more naturally. By partnering with a parent as writers, both parent and student will gain enjoyment and enthusiasm for writing. It has been said that learning to write is a lesson that lasts a lifetime. Striking the delicate balance to bring out the best in young writers is a task that teachers encounter each day. For parents, the answer is found partially in simple acts that we do almost without thinking, putting a pen to paper.

Here is another example of a parent/child journaling. The comfort zone has been established. The parent wrote about a camping trip, while the child writes about swimming. The door of communication is opened by the parent; the child, a first grader, walks through it. The stage has been set for writing together.

"My Favorite Outside Activity"

Parent entry:

My favorite outside activity is going for walks in shallow creeks with my family. It is a very enjoyable, stress-free, and peaceful thing to do. Now that my kids are getting older and need less help (i.e., hand-holding), I enjoy it more. I love to watch their expressions as we make discoveries in the water—like water spiders, minnows, and shiny rocks. It's fun to laugh with one another when we slip or when the water suddenly is up to our knees.

When we go camping (another favorite outdoor activity), one of the first things we do is go exploring—with the hopes of finding that perfect stream—waiting for us to hike in it and enjoy all its beautiful surroundings. I hope my kids come to enjoy it as much as I do!

Child response (grade 1):

One of my favorite things to do is...go swimming! I love it because I doing handstands and jumping in! Diving is fun. (but tricky) Swimming is great!!

Simple writing actions carried out each day indicate value and worth in the eyes of a child. This nonverbal emphasis or lack of emphasis on the written word may well determine what kind of writing abilities students aspire to. The seemingly imperceptible values we place on written words speak volumes. What then, if time and attention are given regularly to mentor young writers in such small ways?

The benefit can impact every facet of their education. They become thinkers in every area of their educational life. Although writing education ultimately begins at home, well before students reach their first classroom, it should continue with parents modeling writing in various ways. When a parent does not model writing, the child receives a clear signal that writing is not important. When a parent routinely models writing in the parent's daily life, the child receives clear signals that writing has value, and a writing bond is formed between parent and child. In the classroom, it is incumbent on educators to build in opportunities for parents to become involved in the child's writing life and to support the child's writing efforts.

Read this life lesson from the parent of a fifth grade student. This would have been a difficult conversation to have together, but the act of writing it eases the way for the partners. One could never teach this in the classroom, the depth and feeling, shared in this piece:

Parent entry:

My hero is my mother. The definition of a hero is someone that is admired for their courage. My mother was diagnosed with cancer far too late for the doctors to help cure her. She was told she could have treatment with awful side effects that could help her live longer. That is what she chose to do.

Child response (grade 5):

My grandma was a very brave person. She is a hero to both my mom and I.

I remember when I was three, I would go grocery shopping with her a lot. When I was three, I still had a pacifier and I went grocery shopping with her at Tops and a man insulted her about me being too old for a pacifier and my grandma told the man to lose some weight so he pushed her into the shelves of food. My grandma had to go to the hospital.

What a tremendous legacy grandma left behind. Bravery, love, caring, boldness, and faith in better days to come—those are lessons that were not easily taught, but they were captured in a brief writing session between mother and daughter. They remain for all time, a monument of words to a mother, a grandmother who impacted her family and changed them forever as she fought to live. No textbook can teach that lesson.

The foundations of writing instruction should be learned "by heart," which is not to imply the rote methodology, but rather a passion for the craft. If this instruction does not begin in the home, then certainly, it should be and can easily be fully supported in the home by parents. A parent is the child's first teacher of life skills and cultural pursuits. Why not writing?

By becoming an active participant in the child's writing life, the parent sends the signal that writing is worthwhile and has value. The parent becomes a writing role model for their child and will promote future growth. The hope would be that these children grow up, support the writing efforts of their own children and pass the torch of writing to the next generation. In this way, we create cyclical change and cultivate future generations of people who not only love to write but who are competent writers as well. By reinforcing writing efforts in the classroom through parent involvement, we build a nation of strong writers one classroom at a time.

Further Exploration

1. Educators generally have strong feelings about writing and the teaching of writing. We either love it or hate it. When you recall your childhood and education, what is your earliest memory of writing? What do you remember writing about as a child?

2. We are perhaps our own worst critics. We are constantly seeking to find a better way to teach, a more effective way to reach our students. What are the obstacles that hinder your writing instruction? What step could you take right now to improve the situation?

2

Establishing Parent–Child Writing Partnerships

It's misleading to think of writers as special creatures, word sorcerers who possess some sort of magical knowledge hidden from everyone else. Writers are ordinary people who like to write. They feel the urge to write, and they scratch that itch every chance they get.

— Ralph Fletcher, author

The apple doesn't fall far from the tree. This often-used adage describes a multitude of educational scenarios, but perhaps never is it so true as it is when it comes to writing. Parents, who are avid readers, typically raise children who are readers. Parents, who enjoy writing, are most likely writing when their children are nearby. They are modeling positive writing behaviors in the home. They express positive feelings toward writing, and it stands to reason that their child will share those warm feelings toward writing.

We all know the joy and wonder of reading aloud to a child. Parents know the warmth of sharing a book together, the closeness of two readers enjoying the same experience. Imagine those same warm feelings when sharing ideas through writing. Two hearts thinking on the same thoughts.

Parent entry:

When it thunders, I feel excited and nervous at the same time. I often will immediately turn on the weather channel to see what is going on. Then I watch the lightening and count until it thunders to see how far away it is (that's what I heard you do to find out how many miles away it is by counting "one Mississippi, two Mississippi...etc.").

At night I listen to see which one of the kids will be up first to run into our bed to snuggle under the covers. Often, everybody ends up in our bed—even the dog and cat. Then the storm ends up passing over and we all somehow fall asleep together and manage to fit in the bed. I think most of the time everybody pretends to be scared just so they can sleep in the "big bed."

Child response (grade 5):

When it thunders, I feel is it severe or is it a quick-to-be-over? Sometimes we drive over to the lake and the news people are there. The lightning flashes and the waves are like a car wash. Sometimes I think tornadoes are on the lake because it looks so severe and you can feel the thunder shake the earth.

Writing together is sharing a gift of words between two souls. Whether it is the distance, the elapsed time factor between the writing and the reading, or just the thought process and planning that goes into putting words on paper, there is much to be said for the writing relationship. It goes much deeper than having a conversation; it reaches farther inside the mind and the heart. It's phenomena that I can't explain, but I fully urge others to take part in.

Not too many years ago, I came across a stack of letters that were written between my father and my grandmother when dad was serving in World War II. In an era when phone communication was limited (well before cell phones), the hearts of mother and son were connected by letters winging their way back and forth between the war zone and home. Each had saved their stack of letters, meticulously refolding and placing them back inside their envelopes. They were kept safe, an unmatched family treasure. My grandmother passed away very suddenly, before my father came home for good. The last of those letters were their final conversations.

Years later, after my father's death, I was able to reread the letters and piece together the treasured threads of communication between the grandmother I never knew and a time in dad's life I knew little about. When I first read those letters, I read them in the context of family history, of my father's military travels, and in the context of time that had passed. Knowing how their stories ended, I remember thinking, "What else might you have said if you knew time together was short? What might you have left out"?

Rereading those letters again through the lens of the writer's eye, I am absolutely haunted by the contents. Filled with details of daily life, the oft-mundane stuff that becomes life, here or over there, two hearts remained connected over the years, the very last years of their relationship.

Hello, Fussy; I got a big letter from you today. I had a free hour this morning, so I got my hair cut and then went over to the bowling alley and had a sundae and some pop. It was very hot today. Tonight, just as we went to supper we had a cloudburst, and I got soaked. So I'm sitting here now in my underwear....I have over 30 hours of pilot time in the B-17. I was supposed to solo yesterday. Probably will tomorrow. It's a great ship. I like it very much. *(Donald R. Wade, from a letter dated June 28, 1943)*

There were letters filled with love from home and hope for a safe return, desperate words from a mother missing her boy.

Dear Dotty Boy,

Do you remember when I used to call you my Dotty Boy? I almost wish you were still a little boy, then, you would still be home with me. I had another very welcome letter from you today which has been read and re-read.... Just washed my hair and I'm listening to the "Back Home Hour." Janet, Cecil, and family were here for dinner. We had chicken, mashed potatoes, gravy, fresh green beans, and salad. Ice cream for dessert.

(Valley Wade Murphy, letter, dated November 26, 1943)

It wasn't until my own sons enlisted in the military that I truly understood the value of those letters. Reading the letters again now, with my own sons serving in the military, how connected I feel to this woman that I never met. How fortunate I feel that I have their letters to comfort me now. At the time they were written, the letters were the only lifelines available to keep the ties that bind from being severed. Years later, they serve another purpose, keeping me grounded. Yes, I know the value and power in simple words. I understand the impact of words in forging a bond, strengthening a bond and keeping the parent–child continuum going. Phone calls are wonderful, but written words come from the heart and are cherished by another heart. It is through our words that our souls are set free.

Building Bridges

Words build bridges between souls, and they build future success for students. Long before our children leave us, we can write with them and help them secure a brighter future.

To excel in writing, a child should see their parent writing often, as advised by Don Rothman, director of the Central California Writing Project at University of California at Santa Cruz. Rothman cited the 2003 research of the National Commission on Writing (NCW) in his article, "The Writing Revolution." Rothman is writing teacher and director of the Central California Writing Project at UC Santa Cruz. He sees a critical need for parents to assume a major role in children's development as writers. Rothman states that democracy hinges on literate citizens and offers recommendations for parents.

Rothman's ideas are not time intensive and do not require parents to be expert writers. Rather, he focuses on what could come naturally to parents as coteachers of children working in collaboration with classroom teachers. Rothman advocates parental involvement in education but also particularly in regard to writing assignments, everything from letters to notes to reports for work and articles.

Rothman suggests letting the child see the parent's piece before revision and editing and perhaps asking for suggestions. Demonstrating the value and importance of writing can help the child develop an attitude that writing tasks in school are more than busy work; there is a reason for completing writing assignments and taking the time to revise, edit, and produce a quality, finished piece. He also cautions parents not to obsess over writing errors. The goal is to capture what the child is trying to express, rather than humiliate their efforts at writing. He writes, "Parents should celebrate their child's effort to take risks as a writer, which often means that he or she will make new sorts of errors. That's how people learn to write, so pay attention to the aspirations and the progress you see."

A fourth grade student, one who needs much academic support, finds writing difficult. Because his parents support that effort in the home, the student is willing to take the risk and write:

Parent entry:

My favorite memory of all...on a day like today when Breanne first started playing the violin. She tried so hard and it still sounded so squeaky. Then Paige started to play the flute. She also tried very hard and it still sounded off key. Now Breanne and Paige play in the high school orchestra and band and they both sound beautiful.

Today I sit here and listen to the wonderful sounds coming from Nate's room. The trumpet is much louder than the violin and flute, but the sounds are the same. The same sweet sound of an instrument that will some day sound like angels.

Child response (grade 4):

I think I can play like Breanne and Paige in the story.

There is so much good stuff going on in that simple bit of journaling. The student is getting a very clear message about the value his parents place on music. He is also getting a clear message from his mother that she has expectations for him and has confidence in his ability. That's packing some power into a few short lines. In return, he is clearly expressing that he knows the importance of his sisters' music, and he is willing to try to achieve that level of musicianship. He is also beginning a new life as a writer.

Connecting School and Home

In 2000, a study of family literacy and family writing completed by Julia Wollman-Bonilla, professor of elementary education at Rhode Island College, found that successfully connecting school and home could occur using family message journals. Throughout the study, journal entries were completed by the student during the school day and contained daily writings about school activities. Parents were to respond to the entries each day, which had two benefits: It not only kept them connected to their child's education, it additionally connected the parent and child in the act of writing.

Encouraging every family to write is necessary to maximize student achievement. Nonwriting families, those where neither parent writes for enjoyment, can be given a gentle nudge in the direction of supporting writing efforts in the classroom. A powerful solution and tool is the parent–child partner journal. This is an idea that I developed, based on the journal a dear friend of mine started when she was reaching out to her son, a rather serious boy, who seemed to keep many feelings bottled up. My friend took a simple composition notebook, jotted a heartfelt note to her son with a line encouraging him to write back. She slipped the notebook underneath his pillow and let him discover it. Indeed, the notebook was well received. Almost immediately a response was written by the son and was left underneath her pillow, to be discovered by the mother later. This process of writing/responding continued for quite some time and created a new closeness between the pair.

The success of this mother–son communication came in part from the personal mother-to-son aspect; part came from the element of surprise, one never knowing when the journal would end up under the pillow. The back-and-forth journaling allowed a meeting of the minds in neutral territory, adding to the comfort level. Mother and son shared thoughts that may have been difficult to express face to face. They began to communicate on a new level, as one writer to another writer. My friend happens to be one of these intuitive people who just instinctively know what to do in any given situation. The rest of us are left to our own devices to learn from people like her. This story stayed with me—the power of words jotted down, going back and forth between a parent and a child. Sometime later it became my mission to bring the concept into practice in the classroom.

While taking a course in family literacy, it became evident that typically when one speaks of literacy, the discussion is presumed to be about reading. Writing is the Cinderella of academics, left to sit among the ashes. If the disconnect between reading and writing is ever to be resolved, if we are ever to address literacy completely, writing must be elevated to its proper place in education, one parent child writing team at a time, one written word at a time.

Connecting Generations of Writers

My father-in-law, the late Rev. Gary Sentz, was an evangelist who spent much of his leisure time writing. He spent his life helping others, serving the poor in city missions, in hospitals, and preaching at church summer camp meetings. Although he had only an eighth grade education, he loved writing and spent time daily chronicling his work and his travels. When he would visit, he'd lock himself away for some time in the morning and again at night to compose his thoughts in his notebooks and write some letters to friends. Both the day-to-day and the extraordinary all had a place of importance. Sadly, the notebooks were destroyed in a fire, lost forever, having never been read by the family. Nothing else that was lost in the fire was half as important as the words in those notebooks.

Although my husband's father journaled extensively, he was away much of the time with mission work. His writing was not often modeled in the home. My husband's mother, an art teacher and artist, was busy keeping the home fires burning while his father was saving the impoverished of our world. Her creativity was expressed in chalk drawings and oil paintings. Thus, there was no writing role model, and my husband became the typical nonwriting parent. He would read to our boys whenever I asked or whenever they asked. Writing, however, he would push off onto me, saying, "You're the writer in the family." My husband didn't have the example of writing set before him. It didn't have to be this way, though. If only those journals had been shared as they were being written.

Recently, Jon took up the cause of writing, drawing our sons in to write with him. I've included some pages from my family's journal as an example of what one might expect to see when parents and children journal together. I gave my husband the same directions I give the parents of my students and provided him with the same writing prompts. We are an average family with average struggles and average time constraints. I fight the same homework battles that many other parents do. I let my husband be in charge of enlisting our boys to write with him. My husband chose the prompts, and then chose which boy he would write for and ask for a response from.

The students in my class are elementary students in the intermediate grades. My children are a bit older, so I expected them to be even more hesitant to write. Each took the task to heart, read their father's entry and responded. There is a difference in the voice of each of my young authors. While their pieces are short, it is easy to determine which is the quirky son, which is the often-serious son, who is the risk taker, and which is trying to figure out life in the real world.

What they came up with is very much like what you might see from your students and their families. It is a glimpse into what they think and what they feel. I don't think you can ever get too much of that. Raising children who love to write opens another door of communication, which is a very helpful thing during the teen years.

Parent Entry:

When I was little I was really afraid of flushing the toilet. I don't know whether it was the noise of all the water being sucked into that hole or whether the hole would plug and the water would rise and overflow onto the floor. I remember that it really made my grandmother mad whenever I would use the toilet and then not flush it. Today when I go into one of our bathrooms and find it not flushed I wonder if one of my four sons is experiencing the same fears I had or the(y) are just lazy. I am beginning to believe that it is the latter and I will have to figure out a way to get them to flush every time.

—Jonathan

Child Response:

I believe that some people have weird fears. That's one of them. I have some fears but not like that. I have fears of planes crashing, huge blizzards that kill many people but not flushing the toilet. I think your sons don't feel that flushing the toilet is very important. I don't believe (they're) afraid of flushing the toilet. I'm glad (you're) not scared of flushing the toilet anymore.

—Tom, age 13

Parent Entry:

When it thunders, I feel sad because it makes me think of one of my favorite pets. He was a dog named Comet. The thunder would make Comet go crazy. One time I put him in an old car I had to try to protect him from hurting himself and he tore all the stuffing out of the seats. I put him in the garage once and he ripped the siding off. It finally got so bad that I took him to the vet and the vet gave me a pill to give him half an hour before a storm. It would make him almost go to sleep. We now have a dog whose name is Holly who is not bothered by thunder at all. That is good.

—Jonathan

Child Response:

Watching someone or something you love suffer because of fear is incredibly hard to deal with. The immediate reaction is to try an[d] fix the fear, so your loved one doesn't have to be afraid anymore. You can't fix thunder though, so you turn to anything to try and help. Drugs and medication can sedate the fear in your loved one, but [their] not really the *same person* or thing you fell in love with you fell in love with then. So what's harder to deal with, watching a loved one suffer from fear, or watching your loved one slowly disappear taking the fear with them. Is it worse to see a loved one in a vulnerable terrified state, or to see a loved one sitting inside a medicated shell?... These are questions I hope no one ever has to ask themselves.

—Taylor

Parent entry:

When I was a kid, I like[d] to spend a summer day out in the pasture that was in the side of a hill behind the house I lived in when I lived in Kentucky. There were always cows and heifers that would just lay in the sun and chew their cud. I would have a young one and just lay down with its soft belly as a pillow and just watch the clouds pass by overhead. On one of these occasions, a bull got between me and the fence. I had to take a different route home which took me almost an hour. It was fun but just a little scary, but I made it home safely.

—Jonathan

Child response:

Unlike my father, my summer days, and more importantly summer nights were filled with more active and let's say unruly pursuits. If my crew and I found cows, we tipped them. The clouds we watched were usually created by black powder innards of illegally purchased fireworks. The bulls that came in between us and "the fence" weren't bulls but badges, attached to irate and annoyed cops. What our adventures did have in common with my father's lazy days was the end result. A longer trek home through mud, thorns, creeks and other undesirable terrain after which we ended up at home safe and sound. More importantly we came home a little smarter, a little tougher and always a little more determined to make our next trip even more fun.
—Tyler, age 19

Parent Entry:

Did you ever meet someone famous? I did. I met a woman named Allison Levine. I am a limo driver and I picked her up at the Buffalo Airport and took her to Niagara Falls in Canada where she was going to speak. It turned out that after having two heart surgeries she had climbed the highest peak on seven continents and was the team leader of the first all-woman team to climb Mt. Everest. She also was the first woman to ski and sled across the North Pole. She was an inspirational speaker about what you can do if you set your mind to it and that you can overcome all kinds of obstacles that confront you in life.

—Jonathan

Child Response:

I think it's amazing what the human race can achieve even when confronted with great adversity. People like Levine or even Lance Armstrong achieve so much even when facing setbacks that most never have to endure. I wonder if things like that is what motivates people to do such great things. As for me, I'm not sure if I ever met anyone like that, but I hope one day, people remember me for doing great things.
—Tim, age 23

Author's Note: Two days later, Tim, still reflecting on the journaling with his father, posted this on Twitter: "My father is the hardest working man I know. I hope I will be remembered for doing something great someday."

No Pain, No Gain

Writing with one's child may seem awkward at first. It may seem very much so because as a society we have gotten away from the need to write. Anything that is a new or little-used skill is difficult or awkward at first, until one becomes accustomed to it. That doesn't mean one should not try and master that skill. This never more true than with the craft of writing together. There is no clearer window to the soul than through the words one crafts. There is no surer way to connect than with words.

It should not take the separation of many miles between family members to get that kind of communication to take place. It is never too early to begin. A child as young as a first grader can read and reflect on a parent's writing with competence.

It is never too early to begin encouraging families to write together. It opens the door to exploring ordinary moments, captured in our memory, saved up for another time. A simple writing prompt brought that memory back, allowed the parent to share it, and allowed the child who might not think ever have made the connection together otherwise. Writing together makes parents more reflective as well as children, whatever their age.

Reflective writers are thinkers. Every student must hone their ability to think clearly and communicate their ideas. Adults need to be able to think and express themselves in the global workplace. Thinkers have the skills needed to be successful in every arena of society. All that can begin in your classroom.

Further Exploration

1. Who were the writing role models in your life? What types of writing did they model? How does that compare to the writing you do today? What type of composing do you enjoy?

2. What is the attitude of your student writers toward writing? Considering attitude versus ability of writers, what have you observed? Do you see a connection between attitude and ability?

3

Getting Parents on Your Side

Nulla dies sine linea (Never a day without a line).
— Donald Murray,
Pultizer Prize-winning columnist

It was a crisp October day, not too many months back, and I knew I had finally succeeded. I don't remember where we had been; my husband, two of our four sons, and I were in the car heading home. The sun was brilliant, and it warmed us all. We were nearly home; I remember the moment well. We passed a tree along the road whose form and placement next to road almost always catches my attention, whatever the season. In the fall, I make it a point to notice this particular tree every day when I pass by. It typically changes from green to the most astounding colors virtually over night. At the peak of its transformation, it is a true visual delight that my eye revels in each time I pass it. Words fail me to aptly describe the vibrancy of the red shades and the tinges of yellow-orange that treat the passerby. That day, with sun dancing on the leaves, the tree was breathtaking.

Though I always look forward to seeing the tree, I did not make mention of it on this particular trip. My third son, then 16, remarked at how beautiful the tree was on this day. Before I could even open my mouth, my husband said, "Why don't you write about it?" I could almost hear a heavenly chorus, "ahh ahh, ahh, ahh…." I knew at that very second that all my time spent writing, all my efforts, had culminated in a change not just in me over the years, not just in my children as they became more skilled at the craft, but in my husband as well. His thinking had *changed*. An avid reader though not necessarily a writer, *he* was suggesting my son write. Yahoo! Success was mine! I could have danced home.

Because only 30% of parents of school-age children and only 27% of educators write for enjoyment, the data collected in the survey discussed in Chapter 1 lead to the conclusion that school-age children potentially are at risk for not having adequate writing role models in their lives. The danger in this situation is that they will experience only the barest minimum of interaction with adults who write from the heart, because they love it. That data show that less than 20% of fathers and 45% of mothers of school-age children enjoy writing.

The worst-case scenario is a child who has neither a parent who enjoys writing nor a teacher who enjoys writing. Depending on the succession of teachers, a child could be without a writing role model for the greater part of childhood. Thus the child would not see an emphasis on writing for enjoyment, a dangerous situation, at best, for budding writers.

This thought truly tortured me, almost night and day for several years. With every tick of the clock, I could see minutes and hours slowly draining away. Parents going on about their business, not taking advantage of those precious moments to model writing inside their home. I knew, absolutely knew, that my children could take up the pen at any time and willingly write. I have written always, since their earliest memories. One way or another, I have always been writing this or that. Some pieces have been published, others, not. By default, my children have always had a parent who models writing. Thus, it did not seem odd to anyone, their teachers, their friends, or anyone else that they should write with ease. Perhaps some people think writing is genetic, but I believe it is not; it is learned behavior. It is because of the example that writing need not be feared, but embraced. Writing is what we do. To this day, one son writes song lyrics, one has fiction in his head, one writes poetry, and one is still a sprout. We will always write. It is what we do.

In my soul I know that the absolute love for the craft of composition is the best gift I gave to my sons. I didn't purposely do it. I fell into writing, and they, luckily, just happened to be nearby observing the writing as it happened, reading published pieces here and there. They have inspired many pieces. But I want others to have that gift, to know that passion as well. The way that can happen is if we as educators can embrace writing and encourage parents of our students to write.

The concept of parents and children writing together intrigued me to the point that I decided I would focus on it. By pure instinct, I began to study the issues associated with writing and to think about how that could be changed. Passion for the craft fueled a desire in me to take up this issue and inspire others to write with their children. This was during the time I was completing my coursework for my master's degree in secondary English education. All of the required courses I took dealt with literature and genres. Because of my interest in writing, I elected to take a course in writing instruction that gave me greater breadth in the various philosophies and trends in writing. It was like the mothership calling. I could only think about writing families, families writing.

This was just about the same time my friend told me about journaling back and forth with her son. As I was nearing the end of my master's coursework, I knew with clarity that I would culminate my studies with further research in the field of writing. I began developing this tool that could serve as an opportunity for parents to comfortably model writing in the home. It seemed presumptuous for me, a writing, teaching mom, to wish to rock the writing world with one more ideal—yet, here we are.

Try It, You'll Like It

A classroom composed of 18 fifth grade students at Cloverbank Elementary School, Frontier Central School District piloted this project beginning in September 2008. The concept was introduced at Parent Information Night, with parents of all except four students in attendance. The project was explained to parents and the critical need for a child to have a writing role model in their life was expressed. Parents were told that the project was completely voluntary and students would not be penalized for nonparticipation. Parents were strongly encouraged to take part as their child's writing role model in order for their child to reap maximum benefits from writing instruction at this key juncture in their development as a writer.

Over the course of four weeks, 15 of 18 students participated with their parent(s). Of the students whose parents did not attend information night, only one did not participate in the partner journal project. Other students/families who did not participate cited lack of time as the reason that they did not write together or that their child did not bring the journal home at all. These students were able to partner with a staff member for the duration of the project. Although it would have been preferable for them to write with a parent or other caretaker in the home, it was thought that they would benefit from the opportunity to have an adult writing role model, whether it is a parent or an adult in their school.

The journal project was well received by the parents who participated with their children. In the following year, the participation among families continued in a similar fashion, with the majority of my students writing together with one or both parents. The Parent–Child Journal project used in my fourth and fifth grade classrooms can be easily adapted to accommodate primary grade students as well as secondary-level students. Additional prompts can be created if the teacher wishes to stay within a theme or the students and parents can be given more free rein. The possibilities are endless, but the particulars are really dependent upon the needs of your students and families. Like any educational tool at the teacher's disposal, it must be adapted to meet the needs of students.

One parent commented at the end:

Dear Mrs. Sentz,

Thank you for the writing project. I thought I would not like doing it very much. Writing was never something I enjoyed. I liked doing the journal with [my daughter] very much though. It was easier to do the writing than I thought it would be. We had some good talks on paper….

Sincerely,

[Parent of a fourth grade student]

Teachers must keep in mind that the abilities of student writers will vary greatly from grade to grade. As with reading abilities, each student is an individual with strengths and weaknesses unique to them. Never is this more evident than with writing. Figures 3.1 through 3.6 are additional examples of parent and student journal entries from students ranging from first grade to fifth grade. I have included a number of entries from students at primary and intermediate grades because student abilities vary so greatly within grade levels and between grade levels.

Figure 3.1. Sample Journal Entry: "Summer Fun"

Parent entry:

When I was a kid, I liked to spend a summer day at the beach. We would get up early and pile into the car and head to Sunset Bay. When we arrived at the beach, we would unload the car and set up our area with beach blankets and beach toys and of course our cooler of sandwiches and drinks.

We would spend hours swimming and playing Marco Polo in the water. When we wanted to take a break we would build sand castles and bury each other in the sand. Then we would all eat a picnic lunch and swim a little more. When we finally tired, we would load up the car and head home, and of course, always fell asleep in the car from a long day of fun in the sun.

Child response (first grade):

I like to spend a summer day going swimming at my aunt's house. My mom puts sunscreen all over me. Then I put my floaties on and jump in the pool.

I spend hours swimming and playing with my cousin, Alex, and I also like to play in the sand box. When I get hungry my mom makes hot dogs and corn on the cob. When I'm finally tired my mom takes me home to go to sleep.

Authors note: It is interesting to read these partner pieces about a day of swimming and examine the parallel structure. Although the settings are different, the child mimics the parent's writing. Notice the repetition throughout the piece. Both describe the setting (beach vs. pool). Both talk about what they do when they arrive, when they are hungry, when they get tired. Both authors end with falling asleep/going to sleep.

When reading the entries, it is interesting to note that many of the student writers have a writer's voice that is reminiscent of the parent writer. Genetic? Maybe. Children pick up on our gestures and mannerisms. Our ability to write is no different. It seems they pick up on our writing behaviors and our expressive abilities as well. If we run on, they may also tend to do the same. If we write in stream of consciousness, they may as well. They pick up on our word choice as well as our voice as writers. Like parent, like child.

Figure 3.2. Sample Journal Entry: "My Hero"

Parent entry:

My hero is my grandmother. She passed away when I was 17 years old. Even though I only had her in my life for 17 years she was going to be with me always in my heart. My grandmother had a special way of making all of us feel as though we were her "favorite."

She told the best stories ever and you would never tire of hearing them over and over. She had such a great personality. She was a strong survivor too. She suffered through cancer and diabetes, but you would never know because she was strong in spirit. I believe a little piece of her is within you that is why I gave you your middle name — Lucille, because now she is not only with me, now she is with you.

Child response (third grade):

I would love to meet your grandmother. I am really anxious to know about the stories your grandmother told to you. I feel bad for you that you were only 17 years old when your grandmother died. Your grandmother was probly really nice to you and your sisters. She was a sweetheart problily.

Author's note: The parent opens the door to a bittersweet memory and introduces the child to an important role model from the past. This exchange opens the lines of communication, as well as allows the child to take on a more grownup attitude as empathy is expressed for the parent's loss.

Figures 3.3 through 3.6 are all parents and intermediate-grade students. The students have varying levels as far as length of entry, word choice, etc. What is interesting to note, is the depth of feeling evoked by parent writers and the appropriateness and connectedness of student responses.

Figure 3.3. Sample Journal Entry: "Thunderstorms"

Parent entry:

When it thunders, sometimes I feel comfort. Sometimes I feel afraid. When it is a soft rumbling thunder, it's sort of calming. Makes me want to fall asleep. When I was young my family used to tell me that it was the angels bowling. And when lightning struck it meant they got a strike. When the thunder gets real strong it shakes my house and I get afraid that the things on my wall would fall, but otherwise I think the sound of thunder is nice and comforting.

Child response (fourth grade):

I like my mom's story. I like the sound of thunder too. I am not afraid of thunder. I like to play outside when it rains and thunders.

Author's note: The exchange is brief, but the feelings are strong. The parent admits to having many kinds of feelings when it thunders. The child draws confidence from the parent and expresses positive feelings.

Figure 3.4. Sample Journal Entry:
"Someone I Haven't Seen in a Long Time is …"

Parent entry:

Someone I haven't seen in a long time is my Grandpa "T.P." The "T" stands for Ted and the "P" stands for Patton. My grandpa was one of the most important people in my life. He passed away a few years ago and I think of him every day. T.P. taught me all of the silly things in life. We would always laugh and have a great time. When I was a little girl, I would swim all day with him and my brother and my sister. Spending most of my childhood with him, made me who I am today. I miss his smile and especially his laugh everyday. My grandpa taught me to enjoy life and to laugh as much as possible!

Child response (fifth grade):

My grandma Sue and my papa mean a lot to me as well. They're not dead but someday I'm afraid they will be. They take me everywhere and make my childhood more fun. They love me very much.

Also my grandma Katie helps out too. She helps my mom every time. She's my mom's mom and she lives with us. In case my mom has to work she usually always watches us because she helps out, even when my mom broke her leg. My grandma took her everywhere she needed to go. They both are very helpful. I love them.

Author's note: The relatives mentioned in these entries offer a wealth of additional writing opportunities. It sounds like there is much more to be mined here. The writers could spend many additional entries expanding on these people who played an important role in their lives. They should be encouraged to continue to include them in future journaling and in greater detail. This is good jumping off point for more writing.

Figure 3.5. Sample Journal Entry:
"If I had Magical Powers…"

Parent entry:

If I could have magical powers, I would read people's minds. I think powers of the brain are better than powers of the body. I would also like to be able to see future events. I don't want to know things like the winner of the Super Bowl or the lottery numbers. I want to know when a storm is coming or a natural disaster like an earthquake.

I would use my powers only to do good. I would use them to settle disputes among world leaders and promote peaceful resolutions.

I would warn people on times of danger like the earthquake in Haiti. I would also prevent terror attacks because we would catch them before they happened.

Child response (fifth grade):

If I had magical powers I would want to be able to fly, I can't get hurt, super strength and I would be really fast. I would like these because I could be impossible to catch and I'd be the strongest person alive! I could rescue people and if the robber or villain who has a gun it won't hurt me. Also so no one finds out who I am, I can fly out of the scene in a couple seconds. These are what my magic powers would be.

Author's note: One of the lost arts of childhood, I fear, is the ability to imagine and pretend. What I love most about this partner journal excerpt is that the partners both let themselves go and wander into the realm of imagination. In addition to modeling writing in the home, the art of wondering/pretending/imagining is another area students need support in. In the "reality television world" we live in, wonderment and imagination are in danger of becoming extinct.

Figure 3.6. Sample Journal Entry: "Best Friends Forever"

Parent entry:

My best friend in school was and still is a girl named Chris Marrelli. I met Chrissy in the first grade when I went to Athol Springs school. She introduced herself to me and I remember it like it was yesterday. I recently moved and it was a new school for me and I didn't know anyone. She made my first day better and I wasn't scared anymore. What was even more special is that at the end of the day she was on my school bus. We sat together and then her school bus stop approached. I remember being sad to se her go but very surprised that her house was next to mine! I couldn't have been happier! She actually lived practically in my backyard.

Chrissy is a very special friend; we grew up together through high school and even went away to the same college and were roommates. We have been through happy times, sad times and even shared many life experiences together.

The memory that is most challenging was when her dad died. He was like a second dad to me and I was his nurse in the hospital the night he passed away in the hospital. It was sudden and Chrissy and her family were not there. I was with him when he passed away. I had to call and tell her. It was the hardest thing to do. The good out of that story is Chrissy and her family call me their "angel." It was like it was meant to be when I met her. We have been through all the "walks" in life and I'm very lucky to have a friend like her and even better still friends for 32 years!

Child response (fifth grade):

My best friend is Madison, when I first moved into my new house she came over and asked me to play and we were only like 4 years old that day was the best from now on were are best friends.

Every day I would go to her house and the good thing was she was my neighbor. We would always come up with a new game and would play it for hours! We were best friends. We are still friends and will be forever.

> *Author's note:* This mother–son exchange celebrates the value of first friendships, elevating them to a level of great honor. Mom carefully portrays a valued friendship that continued to be cherished for many years. Not only did she eloquently describe the full circle of being befriended during a hard phase of childhood, she shows the bond couldn't be broken in time as well as the joy of being able to pay back the favor years later. The son clearly exudes sensitivity toward his best friend and has learned much about keeping those early ties in tact.

Factors to Keep in Mind

♦ Preschool students and kindergarten students can also be encouraged to journal with mom and dad. It is never too early to start. The journaling, however, might take the form of the student dictating the work and the parent scribing. This is a positive way for the parent to model writing and share/respond at the same time. It should be noted, however, that the parent should scribe the exact words and not edit for the child.

Scribing is a particularly good strategy to use for students who struggle academically, especially if the issue is getting the words onto the page. There are some students who have brilliant pieces of writing in their head, but they have a hard time transferring the thoughts to the written words. Scribing can give the student confidence and eventually be a springboard to independently writing.

♦ Parents for whom English is a second language may find the task of journaling difficult.

English seems to be one of the most difficult languages to master. Think of all those odd spelling rules we struggle to learn and apply. Because our words are derived from so many other languages, there are many troubling inconsistencies for the language learner. For that reason, it may be especially difficult for second language learners to participate in the project. These parents may be more than willing to assist their child, but find the task more daunting than for the rest of us, depending on the length of time they have been in country.

Would it be acceptable for them to write in their native language? Are you strictly requiring your partner writers to compose in English? If the goal is truly for parents to model composition and the conveyance of ideas in written form, perhaps not all writing must be done in English.

However, if the parents in question are firmly committed to assimilating completely to the American way of life and prefer to write in English, it may be advisable to give those parents additional assistance (see Chapter 6). These are questions you must consider if your students are from families who have immigrated.

- ♦ A parent might hesitate to participate in the journaling project because of their own prior experiences with writing, particularly if their experiences were unpleasant. If they experienced negativity in association with writing, they may be resistant.

There was a time when writing meant little more to me than jotting a card or a note. I didn't feel skilled at writing, and after having been through years of formal education, having written essays and papers that were returned with sometimes rather less-than-discouraging comments. Very few adults today feel competent and confident as writers. For many of us, the word "write" may bring reminders of difficult, boring, tedious writing assignments that carried with it little practical correlation to everyday life (much like some algorithms of advanced mathematics). Assignments returned hemorrhaging red ink might have so discouraged budding writers that now in their adult lives, they fear the very act of composition. There is nothing like the sight of a blank sheet of paper and a pen that the ability to transport a writer instantaneously, back to a moment in time when a writing assignment was poorly received. No one wants to go back to painful memories, the shame of rejection or harsh criticism. Any writer who ever experienced such—think of Ralphie, in the movie "The Christmas Story" receiving a D as a grade on his essay—can empathize.

- ♦ Finally, there may be the occasional parent who is resistant to participating in any homework/project with their child regardless of the assignment or subject area.

Once in a while you may come across the parent who is not willing to assist their child with schoolwork. These are the educationally detached parents, and they come in varying degrees of detachment. Maybe they do not oversee homework or sign papers. Maybe they don't read with their child (or write with them). These could be the parents who don't show up for meetings, conferences, school events, or anything else related to school. For whatever reason, they view the education of *their* child as being solely *your* job. Perhaps they had negative experiences as a child in school and now have become a virtual brick wall where school is concerned. Perhaps they feel overwhelmed by life's pressures and unable to tackle any other responsibilities. You may be able to reach this parent and change their mind. You may not be able to.

What Do We Do About the Students Whose Parents Will Not Participate?

To fill in or not to fill in as their writing partner, that is the question. It is a decision you must make before launching the journals. I have tried a number of different options for this hurdle to the project. All of these options essentially allow the parent to escape what I see as a crucial responsibility of parenting successful, highly literate students.

Option 1

The teacher can take the responsibility to be the student's writing partner. Depending on the situation of the child, this may be the best option. It does give the child an adult to write with, however, the teacher is already modeling writing for them in the classroom. This option will *not* give the child an additional adult writing role model. It will also *not* give the child the richness of seeing writing valued and carried out in the home. I have done this in the past, although I feel strongly that it gives the parent an easy out. It puts me in the position of letting the parent off the hook and also forces me to usurp part of the parent–child relationship.

Option 2

It may be more acceptable to find another adult within the school setting who is willing to take on the responsibility of serving as a writing role model for the student. This can be a classroom aide, another teacher, maybe one from a previous year, a lunch monitor, a bus driver—anyone who knows the child well and is willing to help the child succeed. This gives a writing role model in addition to the classroom teacher, but again, the child is robbed of the crucial home component.

Option 3

Depending on the situation of the child, there may be a grandparent, aunt, uncle, or even and older sibling who could be called upon to substitute for the parent. This may take a little more investigative work on the part of the teacher to set up, but it is worth the effort. The child has two writing role models in their life and this is closer to the ultimate goal of the child seeing writing carried out and valued in the home.

Option 4

The teacher may simply have the child write in the journal alone, with the hope that the parent may reconsider and begin writing. I never let students skip the journal writing, and I have instructed students to use the prompts and write alone. I only do this if I have spoken to the parent and feel in my heart that they may calm down about the project, reconsider, and actually begin to participate. I have had parents do exactly that. Again this depends on how well the teacher knows and relates to the families of their students. It is not the answer to every reluctant situation.

What Is Not an Option

It is not an option to scrap the entire writing project because a parent or even a handful of parents object or are not willing to participate. I have always had well above 60% of my students and their parents participate in writing together, and generally it is closer to 90% participation. Each time I launch the project, I reflect on the glitches from the year before, think about what I already know about my current class and their families and plan accordingly. I make it as simple as possible and place as much of the responsibility as possible on the student and the parent.

There are simply some things a parent needs to do for their child. Feeding the child and clothing the child are among those responsibilities of the ordinary parent. Writing with the child is a responsibility of the extraordinary parent. The educational value realized from the shared writing experience is so important and so crucial, that one must not do away with the program or allow students/families to opt out because one or two parents do not want to expend the time or the energy in a worthwhile endeavor with their child. Although the teacher cannot ensure the parent–child writing will take place for every student, the teacher must make it available to every student that he or she can. Failure is not an option.

Further Exploration

1. Parents are a valuable, yet underused resource in the classroom. When it comes to writing we must embrace parents as partners in educating students. What is the current level of participation among the parents of your students?

2. What are the current impediments to parent involvement for you? What can you do to encourage parent involvement?

4

Parent–Child Partner Journals

Everybody walks past a thousand story ideas every day. The good writers are the ones who see five or six of them. Most people don't see any.

— Orson Scott Card, author

The Parent–Child Partner Journal Project was designed in the spirit of that first parent–child writing relationship between my friend and her son. By encouraging parents to write with their children, parents are supported and encouraged as they assist their child with schoolwork in a comfortable setting. Parents and children work on easy-to-complete writing activities while breaking new ground together as family writers. The benefits of these activities reach out of the writing notebook to other areas of academic study.

The Parent–Child Partner Journal provides a space to capture partners' responses to weekly writing prompts with the goal of sparking writing interaction between parent and child and facilitating a writing relationship where parent becomes writing role model. The Partner Journal travels back and forth from student to parent and back to school weekly. It contains directions and a set of 20 writing prompts; each prompt facilitates writing and a response to the writing between parent and child. The journal project in its entirety consists of three student questionnaires (beginning-of-year student survey, parent writing survey, and end-of-year student survey), a parent writing inventory (beginning of year), and the Partner Journal. Although there are a good number and variety of prompts, participants are always more than welcome to write on a topic of their own choosing.

The project can be modified so that it best suits the needs of your classroom. Do you want to start early in the year or midway through? Partner Journals can be launched in the beginning of the year as a part of establishing classroom routines, or later in the year as your students build stamina with writing. The Partner Journal can be launched following a particular unit of genre writing, for example, if you are teaching about writing diaries and journals. The options are endless, and you should tailor the project to meet your classroom needs.

Do you want to have your families write once a week for a number of months or do you want them to write nightly for a shorter length of time? There are no right answers. It depends on what you believe will benefit your class the most. Once you are ready to begin using the journals in your classroom, the basic routine goes like this: Parents select a prompt or choose a topic they wish to write about. They can choose alone or together with their child's input. They then spend between five to ten minutes writing an entry, and then the parent gives the journal to their child. The child reads the parent entry, thinks about the writing, and writes a response. The child then shares the writing with their parent, and the partners discuss it together. The journal is returned to school on a specific schedule, at the teacher's discretion.

The reason I suggest writing for a five-minute span of time is very simple and perhaps a little sneaky. I want the task to be as painless as possible and to consume as little time as possible. Surprisingly, a person who writes for five minutes can compose quite a bit of writing. More times than not, parents will spend more than five minutes on this task, but for those hoping to use lack of time as an excuse, setting the time to five minutes makes using time as an excuse more difficult. It is difficult to try and tell your child's teacher that you don't have five minutes each week to spend writing a journal entry for your child's school project. (That is the sneaky part.) I strive to make it nearly impossible for a parent not to participate, at least not without feeling somewhat guilty. I am just not able to believe or accept that a parent does not have five minutes to spend with their child once a week. The only possible circumstances I can imagine would be overseas military deployment, child abandonment, incarceration, or death. In the event of any of those, a guardian is an acceptable substitution. In the absence of those, parents must make the time available to their child.

Ever time conscious, I know that if a parent does spend just five minutes modeling writing for their child, over the course of 30 weeks or so, that parent has given at least 150 minutes of unmatched writing instruction to their child. I'll take that. Sure, I'd love parents to spend much more time writing with their child, but any amount of family writing is going to make a difference. By launching the project with parents first, parents have an opportunity to ask questions. The teacher must take the opportunity at that time to assure parents that their writing is not being graded or necessarily even read by the teacher. The sole purpose of the project is to allow students see that their parents value writing and journaling with them.

On the Launch Pad

Now that you are ready to launch the partner writing journals, take time to think about exactly how you will launch the project with families. Planning is possibly the most time-consuming part of this process. Figure 4.1 is a list of questions to think over and answer before you launch the journals. I can't stress enough this part of the process.

Figure 4.1. Planning for Partner Journals

♦ What is the length of time you will carry out the project?

♦ How often are partners writing? When and how often will you collect journals?

♦ How will you keep track of participation? Sticker chart? Stamps?

♦ What format will be used for journals? Are you making photocopied booklets, retrofitting a composition notebook by gluing on a cover and stapling the directions inside?

♦ Will you provide feedback to the writers?

♦ What about parents who do not participate?

♦ What about students who do not want to participate? Will you allow them to opt out?

♦ When and where will you introduce the project to parents? Open house? Parent conference?

♦ What type of celebration will you culminate with?

Many teachers send home a welcome letter before the school year starts. This is a great time to start whipping up some enthusiasm for the writing year before it starts. I send separate letters to my students and parents. Both get the message that writing is important to me, and that we will do a lot of it. Writing is one of the first things I talk about at Parent Information Night, where I make my first big plea for parent involvement.

The journal is easily created, and can be done in a variety of ways. The first journals I made were small journals. The covers were cardstock sheets folded in half, with blank half sheets inserted between the front and back covers. The number of inside sheets depends on your plan for using them. Are you going to use them for a few weeks? All year? Figure 4.2 suggests more options.

Figure 4.2. Suggestions for Implementing Partner Journals

♦ Send home a welcome letter before school starts. Make mention of the focus on writing together for the year.

♦ Assemble enough journals, one for each student (make some extra journals in case of loss/new student).

♦ Administer Beginning-of-Year Student Survey.

♦ Administer Parent Writing Inventory.

♦ Introduce Partner Journal project to parents. When and where will you do this? Open house? Parent conference?

♦ Send home journals with followup parent letter.

♦ Collect journals weekly.

♦ Periodically send home new writing prompts, parent notes, or other small items of encouragement—stickers, pencils, pens are all a hit!

♦ Administer End-of-Year Student Questionnaire and review results.

♦ Model the procedure for writing entries for parents as well as for students.

♦ Hold an informal, roundtable discussion with the class so students can share feelings and discoveries about writing with each other.

♦ Host a Partner Writing Celebration in the classroom at the end of the year for participants.

A composition notebook with the Write On! cover (Figure 4.3) pasted onto its front can also be used. The directions and the list of prompts (Figure 4.4, page 52) is the first page, leaving lots of pages (Figure 4.5, page 53) to write all year. It is all about what suits the needs of the teacher and the families—no right or wrong way to do it.

Figure 4.3. Parent–Child Partner Journal Cover

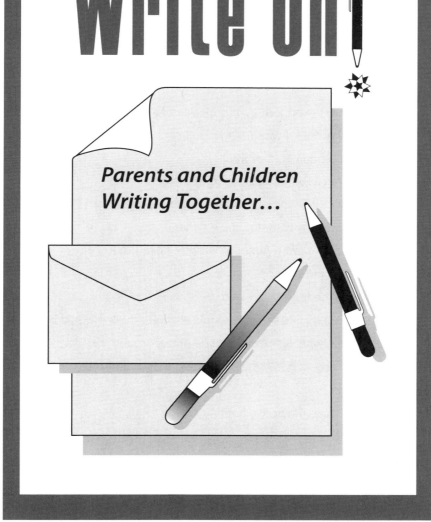

Write On!

Parents and Children
Writing Together...

Figure 4.4. Parent–Child
Partner Journal Writing Prompts

Directions:

Parent Partner: Select a writing topic from the list below. You may choose the topic or decide with your child. Use the first empty page on the Partner side of the journal to write about the topic you have chosen. When you are finished, give the journal to your child so that they may read your entry and write a response.

Student: When your partner has completed his or her entry, please read what he or she has written. You may talk about it together, but be certain to write an appropriate response on the Student side of the journal.

Topics:

- The funniest thing that ever happened to me…
- When I was little, I was really afraid of…
- My best friend in school was…
- When I was a kid, I liked to spend a summer day…
- The most interesting place I ever visited…
- My favorite activity to do on a weekend is…
- Did you ever meet a famous person? I did. I met…
- My favorite birthday present ever…
- If I could time travel, I'd like to visit…
- If I could travel into the future, this is what I think it would be like…
- Sometimes when it is quiet and no one is around, I wonder about…
- If I could write a book about anything, I'd write about…
- My hero is…
- If I could have magical powers, I would…
- My favorite memory of all…
- Something I would like to learn how to do is…
- Someone I haven't seen in a long time is…
- When it thunders, I feel…
- My favorite outside activity is…
- My most favorite pet is/was…

**Figure 4.5. Parent–Child Partner
Journal Sample Blank Page**

Adding a sample journal entry is a nice touch; it can be photocopied and inserted into the front of the journals as a reminder. There are two schools of thought on this. On one hand, a sample can help writers, parent or child, feel confident that they are carrying out the journaling correctly. It may provide a sense of security. On the other hand, having a short sample entry might cause some writers to write a much shorter entry than they otherwise might, the "good enough" mentality.

Here is one that is short, but captures a day at the beach:

Parent entry:

When I was a kid, I liked to spend a summer day at the beach. I loved laying out in the sun and getting a tan. I loved to swim. (I still love to swim.) I think the beach is a very refreshing place to go to. I loved to listen to the waves and I loved playing in the sand. It felt cool on my feet! I loved to make sand castles!

Child response (grade 4):

I love going to the beach too. I love making the sand go in between my feet. My favorite thing when I go to the beach is going in the deeper water. It is very soothing when your there. Once when I was lying on my towel I almost fell asleep because I thought it was so relaxing. I love you so much, Mom!

As stated before, including an example may cause the writers to try and emulate the sample as far as style, length, or writing style. Then again, it can clarify and resolve any confusion about the task at hand. The following is a great example to use with older students:

Parent entry:

The strangest dream I ever had was when I was in middle school. It was the end of the year and I was very stressed about exams. I woke up at 11 p.m. crying and running downstairs to sit with my mother on the couch. My dream/nightmare was that I had to memorize the entire phone book and I couldn't do it! I not only had that dream once, but several more times. I had that same dream every time I was feeling stressed about school.

Child response:

The weirdest dream I've ever had was when I was 7. (Yes I remember!) My dream was that I was a clown at a haunted house. It scared me so much. I thought it was real. I chased people to the exit. I screamed really loud when I chased them. I didn't wake up. I just remembered it in the morning.

Once school begins, there are several more tasks that lie ahead as part of launching family journaling. In addition to assembling the journals, make copies of the surveys (Figures 4.6, page 56, 4.7, page 57, and 4.8, page 58) and have them on hand. Once all the materials are ready and the planning process complete, it's time to get the students involved.

Figure 4.6. Student Questionnaire A (Beginning of Year)

Beginning-of-Year Writer Survey

People use many different tools to write—paper, pens, pencils, computers. Think about the writing you do at school and at home. How do you feel about writing?

Read the following statements. Circle yes or no:

1. Are you an author?	YES	NO
2. Are you a writer?	YES	NO
3. Do you enjoy writing?	YES	NO
4. Do you enjoy sharing your writing with your family?	YES	NO
5. Do you share your writing with your friends?	YES	NO
6. Do you like to publish your writing?	YES	NO

7. What do you like about writing? _____
_____

8. What kind of writing do you like most? _____
_____

9. What is hard for you as a writer? _____
_____

Check the statements that apply to you:

_____ I write for real purposes.

_____ I consider myself a writer.

_____ I write in a journal or diary at home.

_____ I use a computer at home.

_____ I like to revise and edit my writing.

_____ I like to get suggestions from others to improve my writing.

_____ I use words easily when I write.

_____ I am becoming a better writer.

_____ I like to choose my topics for writing.

_____ I am an author.

Figure 4.7. Student Questionnaire B (Beginning of Year)

Parents are Writers

Parents are very busy people. When they are at home, they have many things to do. They take care of us, work at jobs, and keep our home running. Parents are also writers. What kind of writing does your parent (or parents) do?

Put an X by the following if your parent(s) write the following:

Mother	Father	
_____	_____	E-mail
_____	_____	Text messages or Instant Messages
_____	_____	Other computer work
_____	_____	Notes to school
_____	_____	Letters that go in the mail
_____	_____	Journal or Diary
_____	_____	Scrapbook pages
_____	_____	Lists (What kind of list? Write it here.)
_____	_____	Work stuff (like reports, important papers)
_____	_____	Stories
_____	_____	Poems
_____	_____	Articles
_____	_____	Books

Can you think of anything else you have noticed your parents writing? Write it below!

Figure 4.8. Parent Writing Inventory

1. When you are at home, what kind of writing do you do? How often?

2. Do you ever write newspaper or magazine articles? If so, please give details:

3. Do you ever write short stories? Poems, other pieces of creative writing? If so, please give details:

4. Have you ever written a book or novel?

5. What type of writing do you engage in when your child is nearby?

6. Do you assist your child(ren) with writing assignments for school? Why or why not?

7. What other types of writing do you compose?

Perception Becomes Reality

Choose a day early in the school year to get the students started on the project. Before introducing the journal itself, administer Student Questionnaire A (Figure 4.6, page 56) and Student Questionnaire B (Figure 4.7), preferably in two different sittings. The information gathered focuses on student perceptions about themselves as writers. It partially assesses how much writing is modeled in their home and prior knowledge about writing. This is useful data that informs reading and writing instruction through the year.

In reality, Student Questionnaire A is a pretest, designed to assess students' perceptions of themselves as writers and their own writing abilities. Some of the questions are yes/no and can be quickly answered. Other questions are short answer or require checklist-type answers. Question 1 asks "Are you a writer?" whereas question 2 asks, "Are you an author?" I make the distinction between writer and author because to most, the term *writer* implies composing text, whereas the term *author* seems to imply having shared or published written work with another. Student self-perception is what we are interested in here and this can lead to many interesting discussions with students over time.

When I refer to myself as an author, children always ask if I have published a book. When the answer was "no," some would seem genuinely disappointed. There seems to be a perception that our writing is only important if it is in print on a bookshelf somewhere. Over time we do discuss the difference between writing stories or articles as opposed to books and whether writing is be valued more or less based on publication status. Is a piece of writing less valuable if it is written only for our own eyes? Certainly not!

What They Say

When asked question 7, "What do you like about writing?," students responded in a variety of ways:

- ◆ "I can think about other things besides stuff that is bugging me, like my sister."
- ◆ "I like to write about my life."
- ◆ "I don't really like to write, but maybe I will like it sometime this year."
- ◆ "I like to make stories up that are emaginry [imaginary]."

Young students most often respond favorably to questions about writing. When the topic is of great interest to them, they admit to enjoying it. Our job is to keep that enthusiasm up and keep their momentum going throughout their educational career and beyond. If they love to write, we need to keep that love alive. If they are not as enthused about it, we need to help them develop a passion for writing and build a love of words within them.

See It Their Way

Student Questionnaire B (Figure 4.7, page 57) asks students to mark all the forms of writing they observe their parents taking part in at home. Responses to these questions will help determine students' awareness of parent writing in the home. Making students aware of adult writers in their life is necessary. This checklist helps me assess to what extent students see writing modeled in the home, and gives the teacher a general idea of the amount of support they can expect to receive from parents. Once the presence or absence of a writing role model in the home has been assessed, it is time to prepare to launch the journals.

This part of the project is planting the seed, making students more aware of what they see around them. Awareness of writing and the importance of writing are themes to stress throughout the year. It is what I drum into my students in the hope that one day, long after they have left me, they pick up a pencil or pen and write with their own children. Say it with words; say it with actions. This is how teachers instill in young writers a true love for the craft.

Meet the Parents

It is most advantageous to introduce the Parent–Child Partner Journal at a Parent Information Night or an Open House setting where students are not present or even during parent teacher conferences. Instructions to parents include an overview of the process, the purpose for the activity, and how to complete the parent entry. It may be effective to have parents complete the first entry while they are in the classroom so that any questions may be addressed.

When parents attend Information Night/Open House, it is helpful to give a handout regarding all the housekeeping details of classroom life and curriculum details. Parents can read it at their leisure; the presentation time is needed to spend encouraging parents to become a full partner in their child's education. I spend the bulk of my time addressing the importance of reading in the home and writing in the home. This means more than checking over homework or answering questions about math algorithms, or even quizzing the child on math facts.

Prior to the parents' arrival, leave a copy of the Parent Writing Inventory (Figure 4.8, page 58) on each student's desk. The Parent Inventory is a shorter version of the original survey discussed in Chapter 1 (Figure 1.2, page 11). Parents can fill these out while they are waiting for the meeting to begin. This gives parents a chance to start thinking about writing together as they wait for other parents to arrive. Once the teacher presentation is underway, ease into the Parent–Child Partner Journal Project.

This is the address I give regarding partner writing:

There are two things you can do this year to increase your child's potential for success: read with them and write with them. As your child's first teacher, it is imperative to their success in life that you model reading and writing in the home. These are the two easiest things you can do to ensure their academic progress.

Some of you may not like to write. Please, please do not tell your child that. This is the one time it is acceptable to tell a little white lie. In fact, I urge you to do so, if you are a person who does not enjoy writing. Your child will not be harmed by thinking that you enjoy writing if you do not. They will, however, be greatly impaired as a learner if the example they see in the home is a nonwriting parent. Children are like sponges. They soak up our attitudes and our beliefs. If the attitude we exhibit is that writing is not important, our children will not value it either.

Let me assure you there is one goal for this project: To let your child see that writing is good and pleasurable, something that you, the parent, are fully supportive of. Your entries in the journals are not being graded or assessed in any way. I am not looking at what you write, grading your spelling, or anything like that. I am only interested in building your child as a strong writer.

What you will find over the course of the project is that you will get to know your child in a whole new way. You will learn a lot about them, about their thoughts as you write together during the coming months. Writing is a window to the soul.

So, please, I ask you tonight for three things: (1) Participate in our Partner Journal project. (2) Never, ever tell your children you hate to write, even if you think you do. And (3), if you are a phenomenal, skilled writer, don't make your writing too perfect. Let your kids see that you struggle sometimes too. Once in a while, let them help you make your writing better.

As for the actual pitch to the parents, it is not necessary to use the scripted words. The remarks to parents are for reference, to give teachers a general idea of what they might say. At this point in the presentation, I quickly write something for my audience. I don't spend a lot of time, and I'm willing to let it be a really rough piece of writing. Parents need to see that I'm willing to let them see my writing before it is all polished up. After all, I'm asking them to take the same risk with their child. I ask them to spend five minutes writing in response to my writing, whatever it brings to mind. When they are finished, they have a practice piece under their belt and are feeling more confident. It is most effective if parents see how quickly an entry can be composed. This is an exercise is increasing the parent's comfort level.

This is a great time for the teacher to reinforce the idea that the parent's writing is not being judged or graded in any way. This is all about setting ideas down on the page. Parents can sometimes be a bit hesitant about sending their writing to school. It is necessary to reassure them that there will be no red pen on their writing. The teacher should tell parents they won't read the parents' writing if they wish it to be kept private. The journal, after all, is really a pact between two writers, a new, more personal way to communicate with their child. It is really only necessary to scan journals to determine whether or not the child is writing with the parent.

We Have Liftoff

Finally, the time comes for students to take the journal to their adult writing partner. It is helpful send a letter home with the journal (Figure 4.9) to remind and to reintroduce the journals, particularly if any time has passed between the parent information session and the actual launch date. The parent and child partners have the option of deciding together on a topic or one partner choosing the topic. The process is carried out with students taking the journal to their writing partner. The parent (or other adult) partner completes an entry, the student reads it and writes an appropriate entry on the same prompt. Journals are then returned to school.

Figure 4.9. Parent Letter

Dear Parents,

Welcome to an exciting chapter in your child's education! This year your child will be embarking on a journey in writing that will set the stage for all their future educational success. In our classroom, we will be learning and practicing new strategies that will make us better writers. We will be spending at least an hour each day improving our writing skills.

Most of the time, all that will be required on your part is to make sure your child has a space that he or she enjoys and is comfortable, and that your child is able to spend a few minutes each day writing in his or her writer's notebook.

Your assistance is necessary, however, as we begin our Parent–Child Partner Journals. These journals have been designed for you and your child to share the craft of writing together. Your part is simple:

1. Choose a writing prompt from the list (or choose your own topic).

2. Write for approximately five to ten minutes in the journal.

3. Give the journal to your child to write a response.

4. Read your child's writing and discuss it together briefly.

The goal of this project is to spend time together writing solely for enjoyment. We are not worrying about correcting spelling, grammar, or punctuation. We are only focusing on conveying ideas and communicating with each other.

I appreciate your willingness to participate in this project with your child. The amount of time needed is small—five to ten minutes, once a week. You will learn all kinds of things about your child, and they will learn about you. As you display a positive attitude toward writing and model enthusiasm for the craft, your child will develop this same positive attitude. This will set the tone for many years of good writing habits and skills that will benefit your child throughout his or her entire education in every subject area.

Thank you again for support and participation. Happy writing!

Sincerely,

Maintaining the Momentum

Periodically, it is helpful to send a note home to parents, thanking them for their participation and encouraging them to keep going. It is always a challenge to keep the momentum of the partners going and continue building writing stamina. It's like anything else in life, for example, a diet. It's all well and good in the beginning, when the excitement of beginning something new is fresh. As time marches along, it is imperative to keep the enthusiasm up, lest discouragement set in. It's too easy for the dieter to fall off the wagon and eat that cookie. Parents and students alike need to see rewards for their efforts and they need to be reminded of the long-term goal, the reason they are exuding all this energy.

Sometimes it is nice to send stickers or bookmarks home as a treat for writers. Pencils and pens can be a nice incentive. Fourth graders enjoy using a pen for their writing. They will write a novel if the end reward is a pen. Penny candy can be sent home for each writing partner. The treats don't have to be huge, but parents do feel further encouraged when they know you appreciate what they do. Any time of reward, incentive or praise you can give, further ensures the success of the Partner Journal project. Little things mean a lot and help keep the writing flowing.

Wrapping It Up

Over the course of the project, students and parents have the opportunity to write, read, and respond to the other's work. The final week's prompt will be given by the teacher on the last week: "What was your favorite writing piece in this journal and why? Which piece of your partner's did you most enjoy reading?" The student is given sufficient time to look over the entries and respond to the teacher's prompt in writing. This provides an opportunity for reflection and additional positive feedback from both parties.

The following is a sample reflective piece written by a student at the end of the year, along with the parent's response.

Student reflection:

My favorite piece was when my mom wrote about thunderstorms. I did not know she ever felt afraid of anything. I feel like I won't always be afraid. Maybe I'll stop being afraid when I get bigger. I probly will. That is good to know about how we are like each other.

Parent's response:

I loved writing with you this year. I feel like we know so much about each other now. My favorite piece that I wrote was when I wrote about my best friend, Melanie. I hadn't thought about her in a long time. I find myself wondering where she is now. Maybe I'll try to find her one of these days. That would be something. Will you keep writing with me even after school ends this year? I'd like that a lot.

Additionally, the teacher should administer Student Questionnaire C (Figure 4.10) at the end of the year. This is my posttest and gives a wealth of information on student perceptions of themselves as writers. Part C consists of variety of questions: yes/no, short answer, and statement checklist. It is the same as the beginning questionnaire. The questions will assess students' perception of themselves as a writer, to what extent they enjoy writing, in other words, their attitude about writing. The goal is for students to realize a change in their self, their growth as a real writer. Not only do we see a progression in student writing abilities during the year, a definite change in how students view writing, and how they perceive themselves as a writer. This additionally helps inform plans for future writing instruction the following year.

Figure 4.10. Student Questionnaire C

End-of-Year Writer Survey

We've done a lot of writing this year in our class. Think about yourself as a writer. How do you feel about writing? Have you changed this year?

Read the following statements. Circle yes or no:

1. Are you an author?	YES	NO
2. Are you a writer?	YES	NO
3. Do you enjoy writing?	YES	NO
4. Do you enjoy sharing your writing with your family?	YES	NO
5. Do you share your writing with your friends?	YES	NO
6. Do you like to publish your writing?	YES	NO

7. What do you like about writing? _____

_____

8. What kind of writing do you like most? _____

_____

9. What is hard for you as a writer? _____

_____

Check the statements that apply to you:

_____ I write for real purposes.

_____ I consider myself a writer.

_____ I write in a journal or diary at home.

_____ I use a computer at home.

_____ I like to revise and edit my writing.

_____ I like to get suggestions from others to improve my writing.

_____ I use words easily when I write.

_____ I am becoming a better writer.

_____ I like to choose my topics for writing.

_____ I am an author.

At the end of the year is an ideal time to have a culminating Writer's Celebration in your classroom, inviting the writing partners to attend. It can be as simple or as elaborate as desired. Teachers may wish to serve snack food or just share the writing. It is advisable to collect final copies of writing pieces throughout the year and save them for this final celebration. These can be pulled out just before the celebration along with the students' writer notebooks and the Parent–Child Partner Journals. Give students a fairly good chunk of time to look over all that they have written. They are generally astonished at how much they have written. By giving them advance time to reflect prior to the celebration, they can plan for a thoughtful conversation during the culminating event.

This compilation of writing is akin to assembling a great treasure trove of words and ideas. It is a wonderful experience to watch writers looking over the texts they have produced, reminiscing, sharing, and discussing. The teacher who has taught students and parents to enjoy writing together has made a tremendous contribution to the community of writers.

Reflection Questions
(After Implementation of Journals)

1. Now that you have launched Partner Journals, what have you observed about writing in your classroom?

2. How many students/parents participated? How can you increase this level next time?

3. How was the journal project received by parents? Favorably? Unfavorably? How can you improve on this?

4. What did you observe about your students during the process? How did their writing change? Did their attitude change?

5. What could be changed/altered to make the journaling more effective? What else will you do differently in the future?

5

Partner Scrapbook

I admire anybody who has the guts to write anything at all.
— E. B. White

Keeping writing fun and fresh can seem to be a challenge, but not if you think outside the page. Whatever you can do to keep the interest level up month to month while still reinforcing the instruction will definitely make your job easier. Most teachers are experts at piggybacking on whatever the latest craze among our students is. In the case of writing, look to what many moms across America have embraced—the scrapbook. The scrapbook industry has been flourishing for a number of years now because memories are precious. Parents want to preserve them stylishly. A much underused component of the scrapbook is the journaling aspect. Writing…ah, that tricky, ticklish, difficult, and very necessary part of capturing the memory.

Here is a piece I was adding to my son's scrapbook when I conceived the idea for the student writing scrapbook. He had written this piece for school about his favorite coat, and I was placing it in his scrapbook beside a photo of him wearing the coat. I had never given the coat much thought, but I was glad to have a photo of it once I read the piece. It is impossible to pinpoint where inspiration for writing will come from.

"Childhood Treasures"
by Taylor Sentz

Every child has a possession that is cherished throughout their childhood. This item usually is one that brings comfort to a child. To some it may be a teddy bear that was always a reliable friend to snuggle up with. Others may cherish the "flashy" jewelry that every grandmother seems to have an abundance of to pass down. However, my Childhood Treasure is unique in some sense because of it simplicity. Not a bear, or a necklace, my treasure was simply a coat.

This coat, now referred to as "Old Blue" was a navy blue winter jacket. However in its prime, this noble old friend had not received the credit it deserved. As a child it was just a coat, nothing more to my primitive mindset. It was not until a few years ago, when my mother was rifling through the storage room that I saw my faithful old friend. It was a rush of nostalgia, my mind was whipped back into a whirlwind of memory. Every brisk-weathered adventure I had taken as a child, I was accompanied by none other than "Old Blue" himself. Through wind, rain, sleet, and snow "Old Blue" was always there.

It seemed as though Blue's color faded with my youth. Although slightly frayed and clearly worn, he did not look like a sad excuse for a coat. No, Blue retained a look of wisdom. He had not been a treasure in my eyes at the time of his utility. However as I matured, I appreciated the warm embrace he had offered me every time I slipped my tiny arms into him. The day came when "Old Blue" left me, making his way to Good Will. I was not sad, only hopeful that he could provide another child the same warmth and happiness he had bestowed upon me.

Many years have passed since the last time I wore my dear old friend. "Old Blue" was simple yes, but more than just a coat. To this day when asked about a "childhood treasure" not a single item stands next to "Old Blue". Although I no longer have "Old Blue" as a possession to cherish, I will <u>always</u> have his memory.

That was the moment it occurred to me that all the amazing student writing done throughout the school year should absolutely be captured in a scrapbook or a memory book of some type. Who says kids can't "scrap" their school year? What better way to reinforce the writing we've done during the month by using it as a remembrance of the year? What better way to ease parents into writing with their children and engage parents than by working on a page a month together! Ten months of sample scrapbook pages for students to begin and take home for families complete together will certainly keep the writing flowing. The journaling aspect of the pages inspires students and parents to reflect and document the school year.

The Partner Scrapbook can become a cherished memory of the school year. The format is relatively simple and easily adapted to whatever you have going on in class. Although the Partner journal begins with the parent writing first, the partner scrapbook begins at school with the student taking the lead. The student completes his or her portion, then takes it home to have the parent review it and add to it. Again, planning ahead and letting parents know in advance that this task will be coming does a lot to alleviate parent worries. Parents are, for the greater part, willing to participate in their child's education. The easier we make it for them and the more enjoyable the task, the better the odds are that parents will tackle the chore. The trick is to make it seem less like a chore.

Although it is sometimes preferable to have students type the work that will become part of the scrapbook, I think it is easier to let them handwrite their words. Handwritten work has a child-produced look, not so polished and professional looking. Such work carries with it the erasure marks, the cross-outs, and misspellings that were the signature trademarks of the child who created it. The hope is that this scrapbook will find its way into the students' box of childhood treasures, keepsakes that one day are opened and reflected upon.

Use each month's page to reinforce the form of writing worked on during the month. For example, the September page contains a small moment, a vivid memory from the first month of school. Students complete the "journaling," to use a scrapbooking term, writing about a small moment from the first month of school. This reinforces what was worked on during the month, giving one more fun opportunity to put those writing skills we just learned, into place. We need students to see, early on, that they can transfer those skills to other projects. We don't leave that learning in the classroom. We take it home with us.

The scrapbook pages also lend an opportunity for those students who love to illustrate, decorate and draw, to spend more time doing just that. Let them add stickers and other decorations to the page to personalize it as much as possible. Then it goes home for parents to write a bit and add decorations or photos, if they wish. They can spend all the time they want at home, adding more embellishments. Start it on a Monday, typically, and have students bring it back by Friday. If students keep them longer, pages can get lost and never come back to school.

When students bring the pages back to school, make some time for them to share the completed pages with their classmates. Some are more elaborate than others, but the sharing of the words, the ideas and the thinking about their writing has tremendous educational value. As with the scrapbook pages crafters create Pages are collected after sharing in a hanging file folder (one for each student) until the end of the school year. At that point students assemble the scrapbook pages in order, place a cover on it, and either staple or comb bind the books. This provides yet another opportunity for reflection and is a wonderful end-of-year activity.

One framework for incorporating the scrapbook into writing units follows.

September (Small Moment)

The September pages (Figure 5.1) place the spotlight on the writing of a very tightly focused memory, a small moment. The first page of the scrapbook can include several of these kind of pieces if time allows. Small moments are short because they are tightly focused and because it is the beginning of the year. Students have not yet built up a great deal of writing stamina, particularly in the lower grades.

Here is a bit of a short journal piece written by a fourth grader focused on a special object and her unforgettable moment:

I've had a Jonas pencil since the first day of school. I asked my friend if I could sharpen my pencil with her sharpener. She said "...only if I can sharpen it." I said "okay."

She sharpened my pencil. She said it wouldn't sharpen. When I got it back and it was the size of two parts of my pinky finger. I was so sad.

Now I don't want to put it in the pencil graveyard, but I guess I have to.

Figure 5.1. September Pages

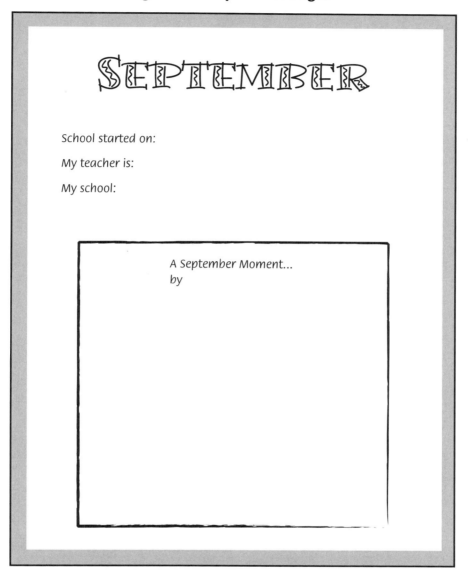

(Front)

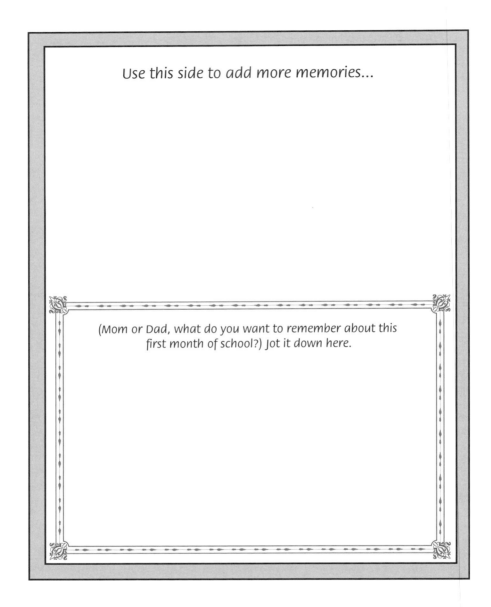

Use this side to add more memories...

(Mom or Dad, what do you want to remember about this
first month of school?) Jot it down here.

(Back)

October (Narrative)

During this month students write narrative pieces expand our writing and work on adding descriptive language, incorporating dialogue, and writing memorable pieces that hold meaning for the reader. Here is an example:

When I went outside with Brownie (my rabbit) for the first time, it was exciting and nervous of her hopping away. I do not want it to run away so I put a red velvet leash on her furry stomach. It was hot out, so my bunny ended up on my lap eating watery grass. Brownie loves to eat grass.

Brownie came right out of her velvet leash. Good thing there was two people close to me. We all three chased the bunny. We circled the bunny. We out matched the bunny. Then it jumped through us.

We raced to catch the bunny. We could feel the slimy, wet grass between our toes. We ran and water splashed my legs and whipped my feet. The harder I ran the harder it whipped me. Wash, wash, wash. I felt my heart racing when I ran across the bed of thick grass. The sun was beating on me really hard. I felt like I was on fire. I took a hard breath and trying to keep Brownie in my sight.

Boom! I caught Brownie. What a relief!

Figure 5.2. October Pages

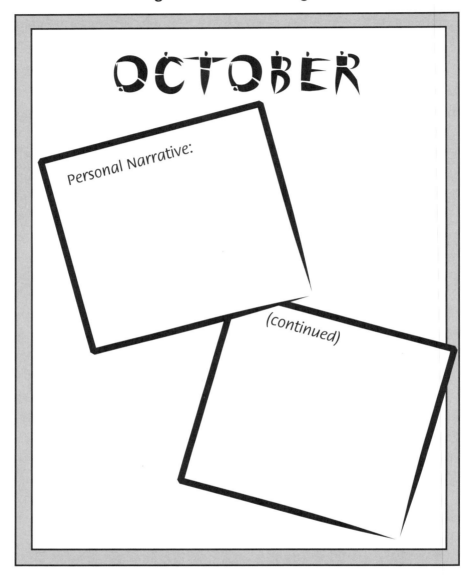

OCTOBER

Personal Narrative:

(continued)

(Front)

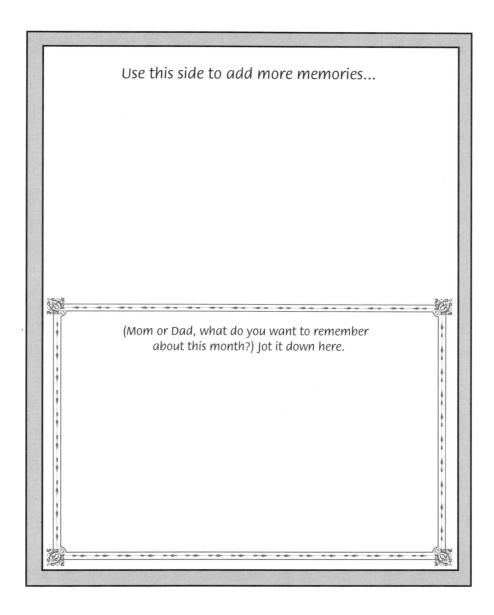

Use this side to add more memories...

(Mom or Dad, what do you want to remember
about this month?) Jot it down here.

(Back)

November (Fiction)

November is a great time work on fiction writing of short stories and novels. The novel writing builds tremendous stamina and the short story writing allows us to work on everything from characterization to setting to plotlines. The final copies of student novels may be completed over the next weeks or months. In the meantime, capturing the essence of the novel on the scrapbook page brings it further to life and celebrates the child's first novel effort, though it may not be completed for some time.

A bit of a first intermediate-level student novel:

Natalie took a short trip to the Big Erie County Library. We had to get ready. Eh, ehhh, ehhh, went Natalie's bright, hot pink alarm clock. It woke Natalie up right away because it was as loud as a hyena laughing (they laugh super loud!).
Natalie threw her green and white with flowers covers on the creamy white fluffy rug....
The shower water was as cold as vanilla ice cream on a hot summer day.

The attention to descriptive language brings the level of writing up a notch in the beginning snippet of this student novel. The contrast of cold vanilla ice cream and a hot, hot day evoke strong memories and makes for great reading. The writing of novels allows students to work on a piece at their own pace throughout the month, but capturing a bit of it for the scrapbook allows for the skill of summarizing and prioritizing. They choose the bit for the page. They summarize, a very necessary skill for students.

Figure 5.3. November Pages

NOVEMBER

This month I wrote a novel about...

NaNo WriMo
National Novel Writing Month

(Front)

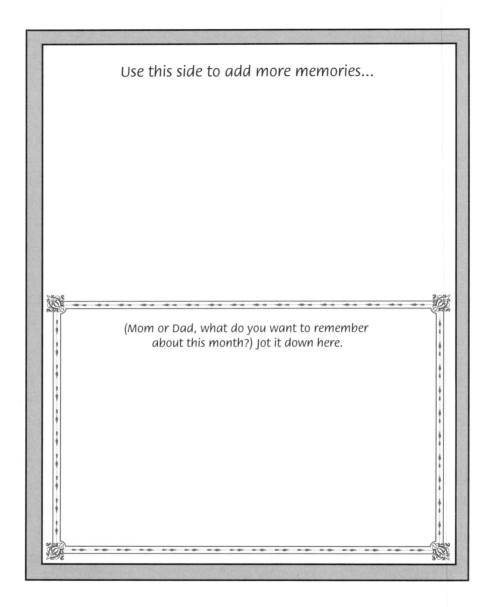

Use this side to add more memories...

(Mom or Dad, what do you want to remember about this month?) Jot it down here.

(Back)

December (Poetry)

Poetry is an expansive genre, it could be the basis for an entire scrapbook, instead of just one month's pages. Whatever form of poetry you teach, this makes for a fun, quick page to complete, even during the mad holiday rush. With greeting cards flying, and holiday favorites such as Clement C. Moore's famous poem, "Twas the Night Before Christmas," December is a favorite month to focus on the writing of poetry.

Read this "Night Before Christmas" spinoff:

'Twas the night before Christmas and Santa was getting all geared up.
I was home wishing he'd bring me a pup;
All the stockings were hung by the chimney with glee,
In hopes that St. Nicholas soon would be free!
Outside my window I heard lots of noise;
I thought for a minute it must be some boys;
Then I heard the sounds of the reindeer;
Santa was coming nearer and nearer;
I went down my stairs to have a quick peek;
I had to be quiet and really sneak;
Santa was filling the stockings up;
And there in the middle was my brand new pup;
As Santa and the reindeer were flying away,
Fluffy and I just started to play.

Figure 5.4. December Pages

December

> Oh, poet Tree; Oh, Poet Tree...
> How lovely are your poems...

Copy a favorite poem that you would like to remember below...

(Front)

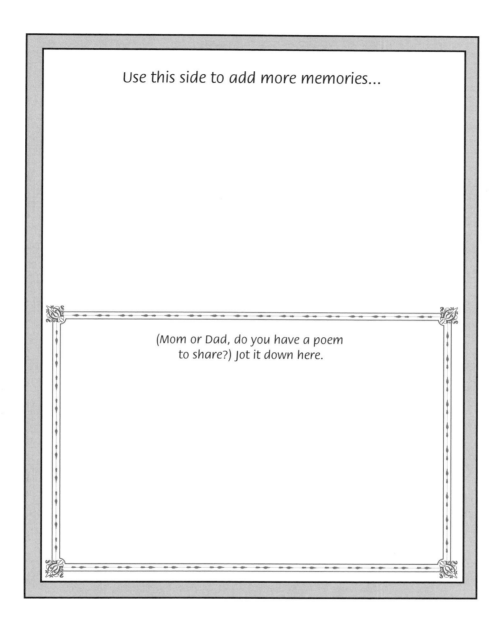

Use this side to add more memories...

(Mom or Dad, do you have a poem
to share?) Jot it down here.

(Back)

January (Personal Essay)

January always feels like a great time to reflect, what with a new year starting and resolutions freshly made. This is the time to tie in and teach personal essays, starting with "I Believe" essays. For the purposes of the scrapbook, the front side of January is simply the list of their belief statements. These are just a few fourth grade "I believe" statements:

I believe...

...All children should have a brother or a sister.

...Kids should get to have whatever birthday present they want.

...Everyone should go outside and play for at least an hour a day.

...School should be four days instead of five and vacations should be longer.

...Families should eat dinner together.

...Cigarettes should be illegal.

...Cigarette companies should be closed.

The page of these simple, thoughtful beliefs are enough to generate weeks of conversation, weeks of writing in the parent–child journal. Whenever possible I try to have children writing purposeful, meaningful pieces that not only satisfy the curriculum requirements, but also advance their thinking. Even more important than hitting the marks in the curriculum is the educational value of teaching our students to think. They come away from essay writing just a bit more able to reason, which means I've done my job that day.

Figure 5.5. January Pages

January

This I believe...

My thesis statement for my personal essay:

(Front)

Use this side to add more memories...

(Mom or Dad, what do you believe?)
Jot it down here.

(Back)

February (Mystery)

Although we spend the month studying the nuances of reading and writing mystery stories, we have to shrink that learning down to fit on our page. This month we write a one-minute mystery or a lateral thinking puzzle for our page. Of course, February would be a fine time to create an "I Love" kind of page. It is all about what you are writing or what you choose to reinforce. Special projects or events could be highlighted in place of a writing themed page. Mom and daughter share a love-filled memory:

Parent entry:

My favorite memory is when I had you and your sister. I remember holding you and thinking that I couldn't believe you were mine. I used to just hold you for hours. Now I think the best part of when I had Julia was the look on your face the first time you held her. You were so proud of being a big sister. So my favorite memory is when you and your sister came into my life.

Child response (grade 4):

My favorite memory is you having Julia because we all had fun and she was a pal, or as I say, my only sister who loves me.

Figure 5.6. February Pages

(Front)

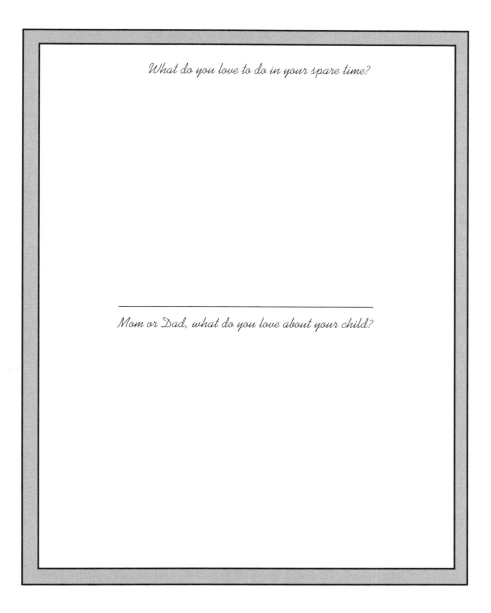

What do you love to do in your spare time?

Mom or Dad, what do you love about your child?

(Back)

March (Memoir)

By the time March rolls around, I am hoping to see students using the strategies we learned in the early months of the year and apply them to what they will write in the future. We write our life story in March. Believe me, fourth graders have a lot of life experience and are ready to share it. They have some very thoughtful insights about what is important in life even though they are only 10 years old.

For the March page, they don't necessarily have space to write their entire memoir, but they can do a "sales pitch" for their memoir. I have them write a piece introducing the memoir. Although the task is to generate interest to a potential reader, my objective is to have them reflect on the writing and think about whether they need to make changes before we record the final copies.

Ladies, ladies, ladies. Have you ever thought about dancing? Do you wonder if you have what it takes to be a dancer? If you have asked your self these kinds of things, then you should my new book. It's called Lindsey: My Life as a Dancer.

In this brand new book, written by me, you will find all about costumes, practices and recitals. You will probably decide to be a dancer after you read my book. I love to dance! You probably figured that out already.

Figure 5.7. March Pages

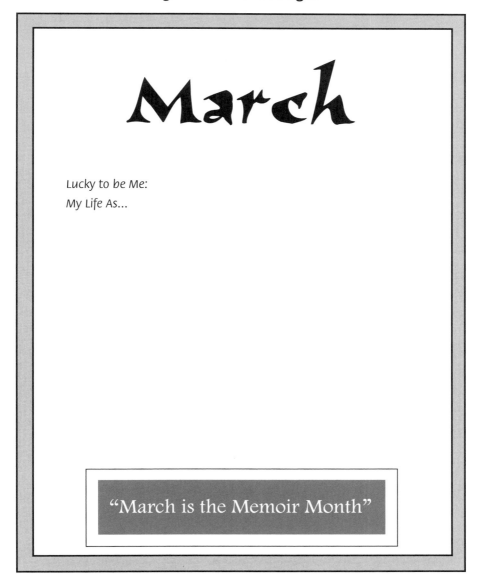

March

Lucky to be Me:
My Life As...

"March is the Memoir Month"

(Front)

Do you feel lucky?

(Back)

April (Spring)

Spring lends itself to all kinds of writing opportunities. Topics for this month can include:

♦ Spring has sprung…or has it?

♦ April Fool: the best trick someone ever played on me…

♦ Earth Day: 20 ways you can save the Earth…

♦ April showers bring…

Sometimes I let students choose their topic. By this time in the year, it's nice to give them a bit more freedom on their pages. They have become accustomed to the process and are readily creating the pages and bringing them back. The sharing sparks ideas to try out either in notebooks or on the next month's page. It's always amazes me how many different paths students diverge onto even when starting out with the same basic topic.

20 Ways to Save the Earth

Pick up your garbage. Even little scraps of paper add up to a lot of junk. Who wants to live in a junkyard? No one that's who!

Use stuff at least two different ways. Use spaghetti sauce from a jar and save the jar to make a flower holder when you pick flowers. Then use it for something else later.

Save the envelope from junk mail to take a note to school in it. Sometimes my mother makes her grocery list on the back of an old envelope and puts her coupons inside it. That's a good idea I think…

Figure 5.8. April Pages

(Front)

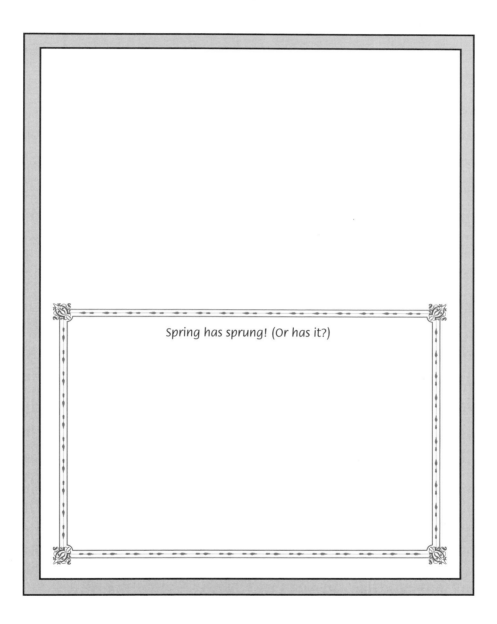

Spring has sprung! (Or has it?)

(Back)

May (Historical Fiction or Biography)

When I think about an All American hero, I think about my brother who went in the Army. I miss him a lot. He went to be a guy who does really hard missions. He knows it might be danger[ous], but he still wanted to do it.

Someday I might want to go to the Army too. I want to be brave like my brother and like my grandpa who used to be a Army guy too. I feel like our family does this stuff to make us all safe. That's good.

Figure 5.9. May Pages

(Front)

Proud to be an American

Ten Reasons to be Proud:

(Back)

June (reflection)

June is a time for wrapping up a long year packed with learning. We reflect on something that has impacted our lives in June. I always secretly hope they will choose a writing piece to reflect on, but it's fine if it is something else. The sky is the limit when students look back over their pages and choose the topic for reflection for their last page.

My favorite writing piece was the memoir. My life as a swimmer was my topic. When I go back and reread it, I think I did a pretty good job and my life is intresting. Maybe not to everybody, but someone who is like me would probaly enjoy it.

One thing they might learn is that being a swimmer is not always fun. Being a swimmer is sometimes hard and being a swimmer makes you work hard to be a winner.

Once they have completed their part of the June page, we put the pages in order and bind them with comb binding. The finished product can be used in a writers' celebration or simply sent home on the last day with well wishes for lots of fabulous future writing.

Figure 5.10. June Pages

June

"Learn Something New Every Day..."

Some things I learned this year:

Favorite Memories of this year:

(Front)

Use this side for autographs of friends, photographs or drawings.

(Back)

6

More Ideas to Strengthen Parent Partners

Writing should lie at the heart of family…if we don't value ourselves on paper, if we don't write to, for, about, and with family members, it must be because we haven't bothered to think deeply about what holds families together. Certainly it should have to do with our cherishing the imperishable voices from our family's past and adding our own voices to theirs.

— Peter Stillman (from his book, *Families Writing*)

One summer day, I was sitting in my car journaling. I didn't have anything particular on my mind, but I thought I would just capture an ordinary moment:

Tom and I are just chillin' at Delaware Park. We dropped Jon off at work and have a little time before Tom's piano lesson. Tom is shooting baskets. He just bounced the ball off a huge tree and is rebounding it. This tree is one that wasn't destroyed by the October storm in 2006. So many of the trees are scarred so badly….

At this point, Tom came bounding back to the car for a drink. When he saw that I was writing in my journal, my real, private journal, he queried me about my topic. I handed my journal over to him and said, "Here. Read it." His eyes almost bugged out. I had never offered up my journal for reading before. He took it, still looking at me cautiously, big brown eyes sparkling with mischief. I'm sure the thought he was about to read some deeply guarded secret. Perhaps he thought I would try to snatch it back before he read anything on the page.

I didn't make a grab for it and he read it, rather intently. Then he made notice of the nearby trees. We chatted about the "October storm," which had been a major weather event in western New York. (It now ranks a close second to our famous Blizzard of '77.) Ice and snow coated the trees still wearing autumn leaves, and the weight of snow and ice on those leaves caused branches, limbs, and whole trees to come down. Some schools were closed for more than a week, roads and neighborhoods were impassable because of fallen wires and branches. Many thousands of homes were damaged, but the oldest, tallest trees took the brunt of it. The park we were sitting in had been particularly hard hit, and eventually would lose more than 200 of the oldest trees. The damage was still quite evident that day, the landscape permanently scarred by the loss. We talked about the evening the storm hit and the ensuing days while we looked at all the misshapen trees and the bare places where trees had once been.

Then Tom asked if he could write in my journal. I said, "Why not?" I thought he might write about the storm, but instead he wrote about his soccer tournament from the previous weekend:

> The game had just begun and you could see Hamburg was there to. Tom, as goalie, had not touched the ball once. Hamburg was taken it (taking it) to them with shots and finally got one in...
>
> Going into the second half, even though Hamburg knew they weren't going to the championship, they were going to make it a game to remember. Goal after goal. The final score was 6-1.
>
> Hamburg showed that they weren't done until the final whistle. They showed what they could do when they worked together. But most of all they showed who was boss.

I thought it very unusual that he would make a leap from the storm-damaged trees to a soccer game. Much later though, I thought a little more intently about what he had written. Although we had been talking about the trees, we had talked a lot about the adversity that had come with the storm for so many people in our area. We had talked about the aftermath and how you keep going when bad things happen. That's when I got the connection between the storm damage and the soccer tournament. His team had not a chance of getting to the tournament championship game. They could have just opted out and spent their morning doing something else. Instead they chose to play the game and play hard. They played as a team and made something good happen. They won big. It didn't change the losses and it didn't change the teams who would compete in the final game. It changed what the boys thought of themselves, though. Not a bad connection for a lazy summer afternoon.

When I think back to that day, I am always reminded how much of the awesomeness of life just happens. It isn't planned out, although I am a big planner. Most of the truly amazing moments are unscripted. They come to life on their own. That's how it is in the classroom, and that's how it can be with parent–child writing. Being open to writing is being open to letting those powerful moments happen. It's a mixture of looking for opportunities to write, while letting the natural flow of the parent–child relationship and writing relationship take it's course.

What else can a parent do to strengthen the love of writing in the home? If we are ever to spark a writing revolution, writing must become at least as important in the life of the family as video games. That's a tall order, from where we stand today. Parents, like students, truly need to be encouraged and nurtured in the craft of writing. If it were up to me, every parent would get to work with a writing coach to boost his or her confidence and help the parent find opportunities to make writing happen in the home. Absent the writing coach, it's up to us to fill in, serve in that capacity for our families.

Encouraging Parents

Author Frank Smith states the case for focusing on self-expression as a writer as opposed to stressing about grammar. In his book about writing, Smith says that it is nearly impossible to "discover anything that accomplished writers have studied or exercises they have practiced" that resulted in their proficiency as a writer. In fact, Smith says, "no writer has ever claimed to have learned [how to write] as a result of the grammar lessons given at school." The craft of writing, true composition of words is not about adhering to rules. It is about the expression of one's thoughts and ideas.

Where the words go once they are on the page is another matter altogether. Are they to be seen by the general public? Are they for our children? Are they for our own eyes only? Only the writer knows. We truly do walk past a thousand stories each day, every one of us does. There is something to be written about in the ordinary moments that make up the fabric of our lives.

There is something to be said about writing about the ordinary moments as you sit in your car. That day in the park with my son comes back clearly when rereading those words. Reading his words about his soccer game brings back not only that game, but other disappointing games that led to one that mattered most in the end.

We lose memories by the truckload because we are no longer a nation of writers. The art of writing letters is different than texting, different than e-mailing, although I am glad we have those communication options. There is something just more intensely personal about written words on an actual piece of paper. It has permanence. At every opportunity we need to encourage parents to write with their family often.

Family Journal

Journals, perhaps the most personal of all forms of writing, are generally only intended to be read by the author. Think about how personal the connection could be among family members that regularly journaled together and shared each other's work. A family journal is perhaps the easiest way to keep writing together. Looking back over the pages, it becomes a walk down memory lane.

Here is a bit from a partner journal that turned into a family journal when the brother of my student joined in the writing:

Father:

If I could go back in time, I would go back to high school. It would be neat to play basketball again knowing what I know now. I also would try much harder to get the best grades I could. It would also be nice to see all my friends once more.

Sister (grade 4):

If I had magic powers I would use them to make something come true and make me not get in trouble. Then I would tell my brother. Then my brother will try to get them.

Brother (grade 7):

If I could go forward in time, I would like to see where I will be in 15 years. I would love to see if I had kids, family or a job. Most of all I would like to see if I was successful or poor.

Vacation Journals

Sometimes families take spectacular vacations or daytrips during school recesses. Another idea to suggest to families to keep writing flowing is sharing the responsibility of capturing vacation memories in a vacation journal. This is a nice option for getting started, testing the journaling waters. A vacation, however brief or long, offers up a multitude of memories no one wants to forget. It can be a daunting task for one vacationer to capture everything, but shared among the family members, it can be manageable.

Another nice thing about vacation journals compiled by multiple vacationers, is that you get multiple viewpoints about the same experience. It is much like looking at the same scene through multiple camera lenses. Because vacations are finite, a vacation journal is a nice way to ease into the art of family journaling. The topic of a vacation is exciting and can entice the most reluctant writer to participate. The vacation journal can be something as simple as a visit to grandma's house.

> The thing I always look for when we visit Nana is that old bridge by the lake. When I see that sorta rusty greenish bridge and feel the whirr of the tires as they go across the metal grate that is the "road." I know we are almost there when I see it and feel it.
>
> I look for the boats on the water. Do those people know I can't wait to see my Nana? Maybe, maybe not. The first thing we did when we got there was run up the driveway. We were making a lot of noise because we were sooo excited to get there.
>
> The second day we went outside to pick blackberries in the yard. We always get to do that. They are so good. Sometimes when we visit there are hickory nuts on the ground, but there weren't any this time. Maybe in the fall we'll get some.

Love Those Letters

Back in the day, letters were all we had. Although today we can barely imagine not being able to instantly contact those we care about, time was, if you wanted to communicate, you had to write to each other. The letters between my father and his mother, previously discussed, is just part of her story.

Born in rural West Virginia in the late 1800s, Valley Waters Wade, never had an easy life. She married my grandfather around 1910 and taught school in a one-room schoolhouse near Mount Morris, Pennsylvania. Some students came to school in warm weather without shoes. Once my grandparents started their family, Valley gave up teaching. Two of her four children died, as did my grandfather and several other family members during the Spanish Flu epidemic of 1918. To keep her children clothed and fed, she moved the family into Morgantown and took in boarders and probably laundry as well.

During those years, raising two small boys, she met a businessman, Frank Murphy, passing through on business, and a spark ignited between them. Because he lived in Buffalo, New York, and traveled for business, the pair corresponded through letters for several years. They must have been some letters, because eventually Frank Murphy convinced Valley to uproot her family, marry him, and move to Buffalo, where they lived happily until his death in the 1930s. Letters between two hearts were the foundation of a happy home and marriage.

Letter writing may be a dying art, but there is nothing like writing a card or a note to fine-tune that organization of thoughts. Letter writing skills are a skill that we need, but one we rarely use. Perhaps because I have had the good fortune to see the positive effect of letters on the recipient, I make a point to write the occasional note when I want to show someone how much I care. A well-composed personal note is worth far more to the recipient than a gift.

A valuable example to set for our children is the writing of notes and letters. Grownups must set the example and personalize holiday cards, jot notes inside greeting cards, write letters to each other periodically. Like journaling together, it adds a dimension of closeness to the relationship that would otherwise be missed out on. Those with friends or relatives that live far away should make it a habit to write letters with the children right alongside. Writing real letters for real purposes opens a world of possibility for young people.

Although some educators promote the creation of made-up letters for assignments, such as "write a letter to the main character…" or "write a letter to the author…," there are endless opportunities to incorporate real letter writing into many areas of the curriculum. If you want students to write how they feel about a book, ask them to write an op-ed piece that expresses just that. If you want them to write to the author about something, have them actually mail that letter (unless the author has passed on, of course). Too often, made-up assignments get half-hearted attempts to complete them. Writing for real purposes and assignments that are for real purposes will always reap more effort from the student, yielding a higher-quality finished piece.

There are also a surprising number of contests that seek student submissions for everything from fiction stories to narrative pieces. Some ask for students to work alone, others ask students to work together as a collaborative team. A quick computer search will yield many opportunities through bookselling companies such as Scholastic Books, as well as many other newspapers, not-for-profit organizations, and the like. The opportunities are out there waiting for your students. Contests and calls for writing submissions really get students excited about the thought of winning—there is something about that type of recognition that fascinates them.

Another great venue is magazines for children and youth. Economic conditions have hit the periodical industry hard for more than a decade, and technology also has had an effect on readership. Magazines keep shutting their doors, yet there is something about holding the printed page in hand. There are still a number of stable publications that offer students the chance to publish. Again, an online search can yield numerous opportunities for our students. Magazines typically require releases signed by parents before accepting any student work.

It's up to teachers to take the lead and find as many opportunities for students to participate in real writing opportunities that exist in the real world. The opportunities are numerous and well worth the time and energy spent ferreting out those gold nuggets of inspiration for student writers.

Parent Writing Guild

Earlier in this book, several possible hurdles to parents writing with children were discussed. Often parent inhibitions toward writing stem from either a real or perceived lack of writing ability on their part, and who wants to spend time feeling like they are failing? Additionally, parents for whom English is a second language may hold back and not wish to participate. Again, it is only human to avoid exposing one's weaknesses to the world.

The obvious solution to combating this hurdle is to increase all parents' confidence in their writing abilities, but particularly to those who we know may hold back. Finding subtle ways to offer writing support for parents could be the gentle encouragement needed to build parent involvement in writing. This support would not necessarily be in the form of a class, because again, parents can feel hesitant. By offering something similar to a support group or a social opportunity that focuses on writing, the comfort level is raised. Establishing a community of parent writers will build support for student writers. By offering a hand to parents, you extend your hand to your students.

The writing debate was fueled further in 1995 when a school administrator in an extremely diverse community in Virginia determined the need to bridge home and school cultures as a necessary component of improved writing instruction for students. Susan Akroyd, then principal at Parklawn Elementary School in Virginia, developed a parent writing program based on family literacy research carried out in the 1980s and early 1990s. Akroyd found that little research had been done on the need for parent modeling in literacy.

Akroyd knew that if parents could not comfortably compose text, they could not model composition skills for their children. To that end, she developed a 10-week writing group for parents of students. As the school population was comprised of a wide range of cultures and abilities as second-language learners, Akroyd knew it was imperative to address the literacy needs of the parents and gain their support. Fifteen of eighteen parent participants completed all 10 weeks of the program, which ultimately resulted in an increase in the value those parents placed on the craft of writing. As with any new program, it began slowly, but grew and became a success as the comfort level of parents increased. Parents who attended would come together to write, read, and revise a piece that would ultimately be for their child.

A gentle nudge in the right direction is enough encouragement to help parents find their voice as a writer. This same approach used with second-language learners could prove equally as effective with parents who lack confidence as a writer. Most parents are willing to do anything they are capable of to help their child succeed. Unfortunately, the majority of adults just do not feel comfortable in the writing realm. We feel terribly inadequate, in fact. It does not have to be that way.

Other Ideas to Share with Parents

The beginning of the year is a great time to share ides for parents to try throughout the year. A packet of information is handy, but it might get tossed aside. Decide what works best for your families: Would they benefit from a monthly calendar of writing activities? Should you send them a weekly reminder? Here a few ideas to spark more writing:

- ◆ *The Gift of Words*—Grandparents, aunts, uncles, and others will appreciate a gift of writing as much, if not more, than a store-bought item. It could be a poem, an essay, a story inside a memory book, on a t-shirt, a mug, or just nicely presented on a piece of paper. Words from the heart are unmatched in value.

- ◆ *Message in a Bottle*—Don't throw it in the ocean! Find a bottle or jar into which you can place a quickly written note. Place the bottle in a spot where your child will find it—for example, near their bed, at their breakfast spot, in the car. Make the finding a complete surprise or a like a search for treasure. Encourage them to write back!

- ◆ *Whiteboard or Fridge*—Many families have a whiteboard somewhere at home for messages, and if not a whiteboard, everyone has a refrigerator. Notes to one another, back and forth, are fun for children, as well as mom and dad. What you write to each other whether it is serious, silly or for information—"School concert, Thursday at 7 p.m."—the point is keeping the lines of communication open. Keep the writing flowing.

- ◆ *Quotable Quotes*—There is just something about a good quotation. Stumbling across a great quote feels like receiving a present. Writers enjoy sharing famous words with others, attached to the bottom of an e-mail, in letters or even just when chatting. Quotes should be shared with our students as well; they give another layer of depth to their literary experiences and give them more words to draw from when writing.

A quote can be used for a lead sentence to start a writing piece or it can be used for an essay. Quotes can become titles or subheadings, names of chapters—the list goes on and on. Perhaps the true value is that they make the writer pause, reflect. Quotes naturally spur deeper thinking. Where the writer goes from a simple quotation is purely an adventure on the page.

Summer Reading and Writing

School is out for summer, but that doesn't mean reading and writing should take a vacation as well. Summer is a great time for reading a book together; in fact, many summer reading programs have cropped up over the years. Additionally, a summer writing program would help decrease summer slide back, the research-documented syndrome where children lose some of the academic gains they have made over the school year.

The writing, if not required by the school as part of a summer literacy program, could be as simple as a diary or the family vacation journal mentioned earlier in this chapter. There is no better time to sit together and compose poetry or begin a tall tale based on summer adventures. It doesn't have to be structured or complicated, but it needs to take place. It is the sharing of ideas, the composition of those ideas on paper on computer, in a journal that make the difference. Although that difference may not be immediately evident, in the long run, time spent writing together is time well spent and a wise investment.

Society often searches for answers to problems and seeks a much more complex solution than is necessary. In the realm of children's literacy, the answer to success may be found at the kitchen table, the family room, or wherever a child completes homework. The concept is simple: write together and write often. The answer is as close as the tip of the pen and a sheet of paper.

7

Bells & Whistles: Additional Classroom Resources

Most of the basic material a writer works with is acquired before the age of fifteen.

— Willa Cather

There is no substitute for good, solid writing, but how you present each genre you teach and the fun factor you put into it directly impacts the enthusiasm of students for the writing. It's like eating at a restaurant. A hamburger is a hamburger, whether you cook it at home or order it at a restaurant. Yet, there is just something about the burger served in the cute basket with a well-placed garnish that makes it look so much more inviting. For kids, wrap that burger in paper, put it in a colorful cardboard box or a fun bag, and call them for dinner! The taste probably doesn't differ between the two, but presentation makes all the difference, kicks it up a notch.

In the classroom, we write poems. Roses are red, violets are blue… Take that poetry unit and stand it on its head, squeeze every drop of intellect possible out of it. Make the poetry unit a bit more rigorous. Instead of writing the same old, same old poetry, have the unit culminate in a final product that takes a bit more effort and intellect such as writing a script for Poetry Theater. Working in writing teams, have students write and perform it, video record it, and share it with others (or save it for an end-of-year celebration). Now you have a project that really inspires young poets to work that much harder. It's all in how you spin it.

There are ten things that you could do immediately—today—to kick the interest in writing up a notch. They take no planning at all, just supplies you probably already have in your classroom and will add immediate impact to your writing instruction and make writing seem less like schoolwork and more like fun:

1. *Colored pencils*—Most students write their pieces in pencil, but who says it has to be a bland, gray pencil? Once in a while, encourage students to write in colored pencil (shades that can be read easily). It spices up the fun factor, just a little!

2. *Pens*—Allow students to use pens for writing class. It makes them feel more grown up, not to mention, pencil smudges as the piece continues to be worked on. Gel pens and pens with inks of varying color make writing, well, a little more colorful. (You'd be surprised how many students will stick to pencil anyway.) Just knowing they *can* use pens, makes it feel like a guilty pleasure!

3. *Markers*—Markers can be used to embellish the title of a piece of writing, used for illustrations, or used to add a colorful border on ordinary notebook paper. It's unbelievable the array of markers that are available. It's not just eight colors any longer.

4. *Die-cut shapes*—If access is available to tools for creating die-cut shapes, there is no end to what can be done with them. Write poems, lists, ideas for future stories—the possibilities are limited only by the imagination. Check the scrapbooking aisle of the craft store or a store that specializes in scrapbooking materials. New products hit the market continually. Students love to embellish, and it is necessary to grab and hold their interest.

5. *Fun notepads or stationary*—Tablets of notepaper are relatively cheap and provide a colorful background for writing. Narrow memo pads which come in all kinds of sizes (available at most "dollar stores" and many craft outlets, often already have lines on them. Writing on a skinny 3-inch by 8-inch sheet or a 6-inch by 8-inch sheet doesn't seem as overwhelming as filling a big blank sheet of notebook paper.

6. *Colorful notebook paper*—Pastel shades of notebook filler paper are more appealing to the writer (and to the reader), and they give students a bit more choice and freedom in how their final piece looks.

7. *Stickers*—Open that drawer full of stickers and let students reward themselves each time they complete their at-home writing. It is nice to let students monitor their own nightly writing, stickering their own work when they achieve their goal. If possible, it is best to establish a no-guilt approach to writing. Stickers also provide a quick fix for artwork if time is an issue.

8. *Stamps*—Stamps and ink pads provide the same thrill for students as stickers. It never gets old. Let students use them to decorate their writing, making colorful borders or an illustration for their work. Stamps can be used when checking in the nightly writing assignment or they can be used to encourage students to write a certain amount. Example: "Write until you reach the star" (or whatever the stamp depicts). The next night they have to continue writing beyond where the stamp is placed. Students can also use them as a self-reward for writing.

9. *Whisper phones*—These PVC wonders are usually used by students for reading aloud, but take on new life as students read their work for purposes of revision and for proofreading their pieces of writing. If you don't have a complete class set or don't have any at all, the directions for constructing them are simple: Take a section of PVC pipe approximately five inches in length. When making a class set, buy a long piece of piping and cut it with a saw. Place elbow sections on each end so that the finished product resembles a telephone. Whisper phones can be purchased through a variety of sources, but they are very inexpensive to make.

10. *Royal Writers*—A notebook is just a notebook, but a Royal Writer Journal, now that is a notebook fit for a king or a queen. Spin the concept of take-home journals into Royal Writers Journals, more specifically Prince and Princess diaries. Talk with students about "royal" words—king, queen, ruler sovereign, emperor, regent, consort, etc. Have students decide what manner of royalty they wish to be. Students then create a title page for their Royal Writer notebook, glue in a symbol that represents royalty—chess piece die cut, fleur-de-lis, etc.—onto the first page of the notebook. Example: "The Royal Writer Journal of Princess Emily." Imagining oneself as royalty just makes the journaling a bit more special. Anything to make it fun and get the imaginations soaring! Who doesn't want to be royalty?

What Else Can You Do?

We all have a curriculum or writing program that we teach by. A program is only the starting point for the expert writing teacher. In my district, we follow Lucy Calkins' methodology. Those familiar with Calkins will notice her influence in the materials and methods I use.

This section has some of the unit material, project ideas, and graphic organizers that have proven effective for teaching writing, as well as templates, source books, websites, and other information to make the writing come alive in your classroom. Some are materials I have created, and some are ideas and materials available for classroom use that I've snagged from the online sources and adapted. Some have their roots in ideas most of us have seen elsewhere. The key is adapting great ideas and making them work for you. This is the hallmark of the innovative educator. Use as a springboard, adapt or use as directed.

A Moment in Time

You never know where inspiration will come from. A perfect inspiration for illustrations to complement the writing-unit-in-progress were found when walking past a recycling bin. It was there in a magazine right on top of the pile, conveniently open to an advertisement for a camera. It was right there staring up at me and it caught my eye. Wham! A lightning bolt of an idea hit me. The unit calls for teaching students to write a "small moment," which is really the start of a narrative piece. When I saw the camera ad, it clicked in my head that a small moment is absolutely what a photograph is—a moment captured.

To complete this piece with your class, ask students to think about a vivid memory they have, then take a photograph of that moment in their mind. This is the basis for the writing piece that will be created over the next week or so.

After going through the process of writing and completing a final copy, have students illustrate the piece using a camera graphic. Place artwork in the camera viewfinder space, and attach the final copy to the camera/illustration. The illustrations can also be done as a partner project with one partner reading the second partner's writing piece, then creating the illustration based on the description within the writing.

NaNo WriMo—National Novel Writing Month

As November approaches, the hearts of novel writers begin to race as we prepare for NaNo WriMo, *National Novel Writing Month*. Imagine writing a novel. Imagine writing that novel in 30 days. Impossible? Not at all. My fourth graders do it every November and so do thousands of other writers across America.

The idea behind NaNo WriMo is for writers to commit to writing everyday, establishing and achieving a daily word count, and writing a novel during the month of November. One objective of NaNo WriMo is for writers to build writing stamina, making writing a habit and push past preconceived notions that there is some magic to novel writing. A countdown poster outside my classroom door 10 days prior to NaNo WriMo piques student interest as they come to class and to others passing by. None of them have ever heard of it, so they buzz with curiosity as the start date comes closer and closer. Students come up with an amazing array of possibilities about what NaNo WriMo could be.

Complete details of NaNo WriMo can be found on the project website as well as many useful tools and ideas for teaching fiction writing. One way to incorporate NaNo WriMo into the curriculum is through a fiction-writing unit. Students can write short stories in class, but work on their novel at home each night for their nightly assignment, working hard to meet their writing goal. It is most effective if the goal is one they have set for themselves. Encourage students to set a reasonable word count that can be achieved in 15 to 20 minutes of writing. Each day when they arrive, have them shade in a square on a word count grid if they have met their goal, placing a small arrow pointing upward if they exceed their goal. Strongly and enthusiastically encourage students to exceed their goals, even if only by a few words. There is a great satisfaction that comes from going above and beyond.

Parents could also be challenged to try their hand at NaNo WriMo, or parents and students could write their novel as a team. Collaboration is a great skill for students to practice and not one easily mastered. What a lovely way to share ideas, over a chapter of fiction! This could spark many conversations about books being read, or books previously read.

Figure 7.1. Daily Goal Graph

Directions: Shade in 1 box, start at the bottom, each time you meet or exceed your NaNo WriMo writing goal in the month of November! Draw an arrow pointing up beside the box if you exceed your goal.

| Day 20 |
| Day 19 |
| Day 18 |
| ... |
| Day 4 |
| Day 3 |
| Day 2 |
| Day 1 |

Students who achieve their NaNo WriMo goal are treated to choosing a special author's pen from my stash of prizes. I reserve a supply of really fun, colorful, cool pens sure to intrigue a young writer specifically for the achievers of NaNo WriMo. Here is a poem inspired by the pen prize:

"Special Pen"
Can't erase
very cool
blue red
white black
got from
writing novel
I use
my pen
every day
since I
got it
here in
my school.

When it comes to classroom writing, it is never immediately known what will be the inspiration for the next piece of writing. Something simple, like a pen, can inspire a child to write. That gives me great encouragement to imagine the possibilities when parents write with their children.

When you visit the NaNo WriMo young writers portion of the site, look for features like the Dare Machine. Click for a "dare" to weave into student writing. Here's one: "We dare you to make a character entirely dependent on fortune cookie fortunes in order to make decisions." Be sure to check out the writers' resources on the page, particularly "Amber's Virtual Library. There are dozens and dozens of sites to glean resources from.

Lists, Lists and More Lists

Some of the writer resources found on the NaNo WriMo website are really handy to have in the classroom. There are lists of 100 first names for characters, both male and female. There are also 100 surnames. To introduce the name lists, try having students write down a number between 1 and 100. Whatever number they pick, they match that number with the number of the name. Students enjoy reading the names. Most are rather unusual, such as Mirabel or Finneus, which makes naming a character just seem that much more inviting. Naming characters has never sparked such interest and such conversation in a classroom before. The characters become unique individuals, which is exactly what we want!

Another idea offered on the website is the plot roller coaster (look for it within the Young Writers workbook, available on the website for free download). I incorporate the roller coaster into a larger graphic organizer with three die cut people forms we use gingerbread people shapes). These represent three characters for the story, one main and two supporting characters; students write each character's description on the shapes. A filmstrip graphic is secured across the bottom of the page for the thumbnail illustrations (see Figure 7.2, page 118)

The site also has lists of plot elements to incorporate, but a word of caution: the teacher *must* screen and selectively use those because some are intended for adult writers. It is advisable to use some of the site resources and add student-generated elements as well when teaching about adding a twist to the plot. Students can also generate lists of street names, cities, towns, and names for pets, when you teach a lesson on nouns or proper nouns, for example. The opportunities are endless when you place your own spin on the resources.

To browse the multitude of writing resources courtesy of NaNo WriMo or to access the numerous links to others sites that offer writing resources, visit: http://ywp.nanowrimo.org.

Handy Transition Words: *First, Next, Then, So, Finally*

A "Lucy" strategy is storytelling the writing piece by holding up a finger each time the writer gets to a transition word. It's almost like counting on your fingers, but substituting the story being created. Using the strategy is effective, but it is made more effective by having students capture it in their notebook. They will remember it better and will see it as they flip back through their notebook.

The storytelling part goes something like this: "First I wiggled my toes out from under the covers. (*hold up your thumb*)" "Next I put my feet on the floor. (*index finger*)" "Then I quickly grabbed my bathrobe. (*middle finger*)" "So I made my way down to the living room. (*ring finger*)" "Finally, we started opening our Christmas presents. (*pinky finger*)"

Have students trace their right hand in their notebook. This can be tricky for the right-handers, but you want a thumb on the left side of the page. Write the transition words on the fingers. Using the transition words above, start with the thumb and have students label each finger as shown in Figure 7.3 on page 119.

Figure 7.2. Plot Roller Coaster with Characters and Filmstrip Thumbnails

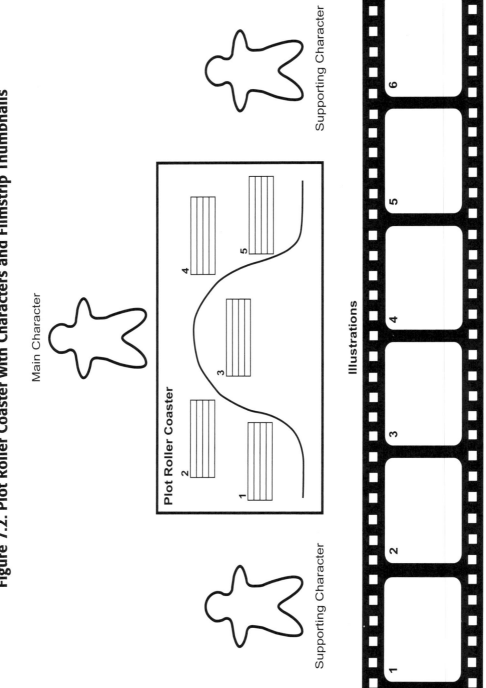

Figure 7.3. Handy Transition Words

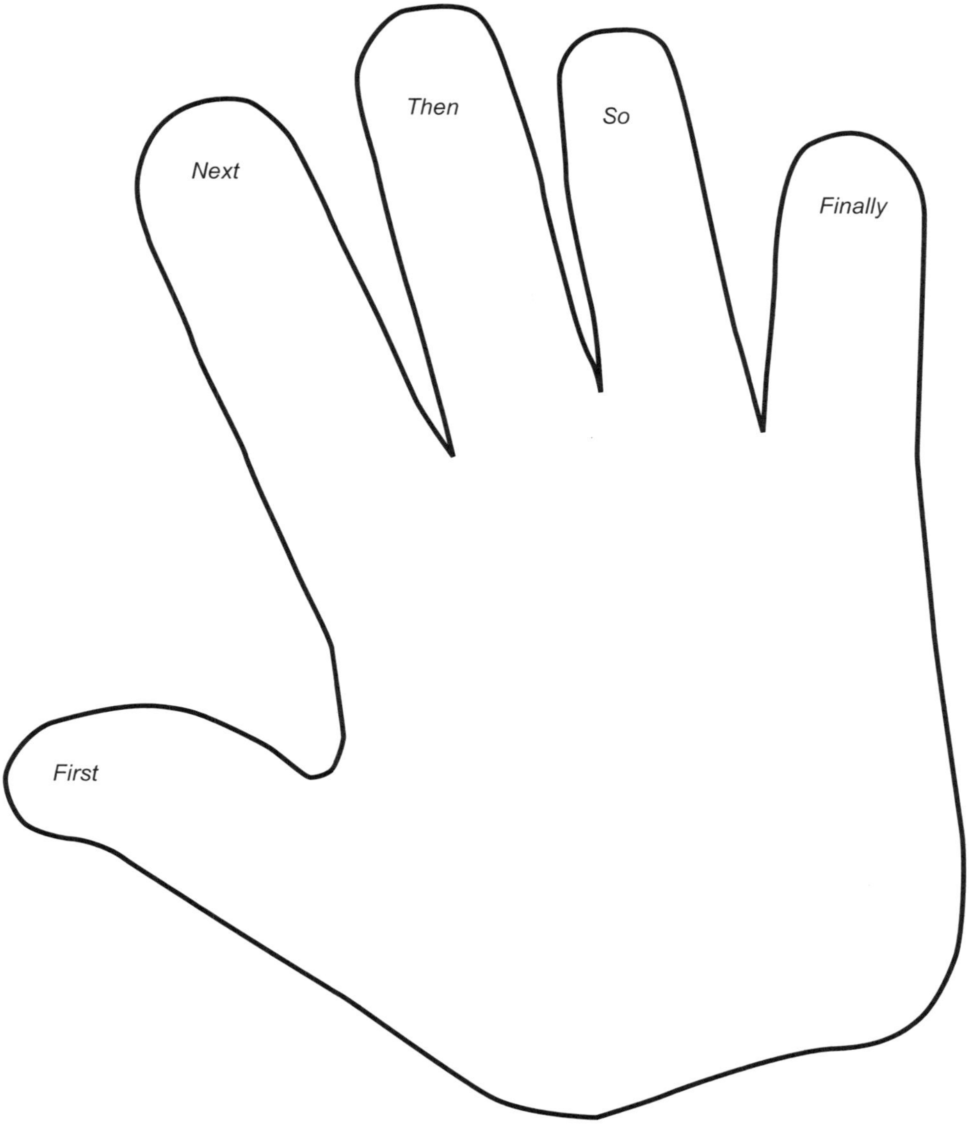

Next

Then

So

Finally

First

Students now have a strategy for thinking the writing through, story-telling it a few times to get the order of the events and the flow of the piece firmly cemented in their minds. Lucy Calkins devised this strategy for transition words; the hand graphic is how students make it their own. Later in the year, the hand strategy can be a springboard to other transition words.

Pump It Up!

This revision strategy is one that is helpful to teach early in the writing year. There is no quicker way to make one's writing better than to get rid of dull words and put spicier ones in their place. Get rid of overused words, such as "nice," "big," or "little." Generate a list of overused/boring words with students. Banish them from your writing. Students copy this in their notebooks:

1. Choose a boring word (can be a noun or a verb)

2. Cross the word out.

3. Pump up your writing by replacing that boring word with a better, more interesting word.

Got Crayons and Paint Chips? Add Some Color to Your Words!

Paint chips from the paint department are a truly beautiful resource for writers. Paint colors have some of the most interesting words attached to them. Paint a room green? Not on your life. Instead, paint your walls and your words "froggy" green, or "fern" green, or "inchworm" green, or "Granny Smith apple" green. Color with a blue crayon? No way. Try "baby cornflower," "cerulean," "faces-in-clouds," "manatee," "shy turquoise," or "sleepover sky" blue.

Have students peruse names written on the paper wrapper of crayons and the names given to colors on paint chips. In the notebook students jot favorite color names—interesting/unusual names—in their notebook along with a swatch of color. Tucked safely in the notebook, they can be referenced easily. When they need to use a color word, they have some examples handy. Keep paint chips and crayons in the writing center where students have access so they can browse the colors whenever they are stuck for a description.

Scene Setters

Speaking of paint chips and resources that are available at home improvement stores, don't overlook those free brochures that show beautifully appointed rooms and list all the paint colors used. Those photographs make awesome settings for a story. The colors are usually quite vivid, and the pictures often contain interesting decorative details.

Students can be instructed to choose one and write a story within that setting or they can be used to jump-start a freewriting session: "Look at the photograph for one minute. Write about what you saw in the photo." This is a quick-and-easy activity that can easily spice up your writing lessons.

Important Things

One of the most impressive projects to do with students is to create a *real* class book. We deal with an actual publishing company that specializes in working with schools and publishing student writing. Every student completes a page and an illustration for the book. The choice of topic is yours. Families can purchase a copy if they so desire. The final copy is a hardcover, bound book that is a treasure for years to come.

Our entire grade level created class books one year in conjunction with our art department. The art teacher assisted students with the illustrations, which were black-and-white photographs of an object that is an "important thing" to the student. In writing class, we completed the text to go alongside each photograph. The end product was striking, not only because of the simplicity of the black-and-white photographs but also because of the choice of object and the strikingly beautiful words the students chose to tell why the object was important.

The publishing company I use supplies everything from postage to paper for the project. The finished book ended up being a truly treasured piece of literature for the classroom. There were many options available for the layout of the book. The topic and theme was mine to choose. The sky is the limit. Watching the students hold the "real," published book and the expressions on their faces was completely magical (and worth the minor headache of assembling everything and meeting the deadline!). Nothing did more to make my students believe in themselves as writers. We did the project early in the year, so they had all year to bask in their published accomplishment. The following piece was written by a student:

Nana's Earrings

My Grama gave me real diamond earrings. Now I can remember her forever. The earrings are shaped like Mickey Mouse's face, but on every side it has my birthstone. When she opened [the box], it shined in the sun. They were so beautiful.

When she dies, I [will] have her in my heart and in my earrings. I love my Nana. She's the best Nana in the world.

Poet Tree Poetry

My mother has a habit of giving me lots of good stuff she doesn't want around her house anymore. Who can say no to such treasure? One such item, an old artificial green, leafy tree, found its way into my classroom. This tree, no longer needed to catch dust, was a perfect accessory for my reading and writing center. Its branches were just sturdy enough to be able to hold poems written by student authors throughout the year. We begin the school year by hanging student bio-poems on it, followed by autumnal pieces.

Two-word line poems—each line has two words describing the topic— are easy to write, so much so, that students love them! They come up with extremely thought-provoking pieces. It isn't the quantity of words; it's the quality. Two-word line poems can be used for any topic. Here are two examples:

My house
is warm,
is loud,
is small,
is fun,
has toys.

"Thunder"
loud, scary
comes with
lightning a
big bang
and there
goes the
power.

The poet tree is sturdy enough to even hold some Christmas lights ornaments and poems during the holiday season. In the spirit of the holidays and in the spirit of recycling, seasonal poems can be written on the back of greeting card illustrations that have been separated from the verse portion. Students enjoy browsing through the card choices to find a perfect illustration for their holiday/winter poem. Encourage students to bring in their holiday cards once the holiday season ends to replenish the supply of recycled card front panels for the following year.

No artificial tree? Create a large paper version and affix to a blank wall space. Instant Poet Tree (and no dusting needed!).

Poetry Theater

If you like Reader's Theater, you will love encouraging your students to write Poetry Theater scripts (Figure 7.4). As a culminating project for a poetry unit, have students use all the knowledge they have gained and all the strategies they have learned and apply that knowledge as they write poetry theater pieces.

Figure 7.4. Sample Poetry Theater Script

"Down the Slide I Go"

Characters:

    Little Girl

    A Playground Slide

Little Girl:	(pretend to slide down the slide) Whhheeee!! Down the slide I go Into the cold and wintry snow
Slide:	(pretend to get scratched by button Ouch! Your buttons hurt Take them off, or I'll blurt!
Little Girl:	Oh! Sorry Slide I'll take them off, with some pride!
Slide:	Thank you little girl. Now, go, and take a little twirl
Little Girl:	(twirls) Goodbye!
Slide:	Goodbye!

The End

Students work together in small groups (three to four students) and develop a plot and characters. Working as a team of writers, they create a script with lines for each character that follows the plot. The scripts must be in poem format. They make props and bring simple costumes if desired and present their poetry theater skits to the class.

Writing poetry theater scripts is a bit challenging as a concept. Working in writing teams steps up the challenge a bit more. Presenting requires students to become fluent in reading their lines, a much-needed skill. Sample scripts can be found at the Giggle poetry site to give the students examples of poetry theater pieces.

Video record each presentation to be enjoyed again at a later time (or uploaded to your teacher website). Classrooms that have an electronic whiteboard in place can use the board to flash scenery behind the presenters. It gives a completely different effect for the audience as they experience student poets at work.

To access Giggle poetry and poetry theater scripts, visit http://www.gigglepoetry.com

Another excellent source if you are searching for examples of poetry when you teach the genre is available at the Can Teach site: http://www.canteach.ca/elementary/songspoems.html#

This, I Believe

What do we believe? The youngest essayist can build a stirring piece of writing based on what they believe. A format that students have great success with when beginning instruction of essays, is "This, I Believe." This is a concept suggested by writer and poet Amy Ludwig Vandewater at a writing conference and is based on the National Public Radio (NPR) listener commentary venue. "This, I Believe" gives students a great opportunity to succeed in the genre because they can, even age the age of 10 years, clearly articulate their beliefs. Students can also give supporting evidence of those beliefs from their lives.

Prewriting tasks include generating a list of "I believe" statements, choosing one to expound upon, and coming up with three examples to support.

I believe…

…everything should be cheaper.

…they should shut down cigarette factories.

…security should be advanced.

…make a stronger substance to build with.

…make stronger glass.

…make longer lasting lightbulbs.

Once the planning is completed, students begin working with the "I believe" statement they selected and write a thesis statement. The thesis statement is based on their belief statement. Insist that the thesis statement be "bigger thinking" and reflect how their belief relates to a wider audience:

I believe my sister is the best birthday gift I ever got.

The thesis statement that was built from the above "I believe" statement is this:

Siblings are people who will be there for you in good times and in bad times.

Students then add two more sentences about the topic, and presto, there is a very fine fourth grade introductory paragraph:

> I believe my sister is the best birthday gift I ever got. Siblings are people who will be there for you in good times and in bad times. Having a sibling is like having a friend who never has to go home. A sibling is your friend forever. My sister has always been my most special friend.

Add three supporting paragraphs and a conclusion, and a personal essay is a breeze.

Pop! Goes the Mystery

Mystery writing is a challenge for the strongest, and this genre is among the most difficult of all the genres for students to tackle. That doesn't mean it should be skipped, avoided, or not tackled. Quite the opposite. Kids love mysteries, and although it can be daunting, there are numerous resources out there to make mystery writing doable in the classroom. Gather up your magnifying glasses, file folders, and as many mystery stories as you can find. (I have a Detective Scooby Doo stuffed animal that I hang on a hook beside my door when the Mystery Unit kicks off.) It's all about fun!

A wealth of information about teaching the mystery genre is available at the Scholastic Books website: www. scholastic.com. You can find complete lessons, games, and other teaching materials for the mystery. Additionally, Scholastic published a book of pop-up story starters a few years ago called *Pop-Up Activities to Teach Genre: 18 Unique Pop-Up Projects with Templates, Story Starters, and Graphic Organizers That Motivate Kids to Write in Different Genres* by Tamara B. Miller. This book contains two pop-ups and organizers, "Mystery at the Manor" and "Mystery Under the Big Top." Mystery writing is painless using the story starter and other materials needed to create a pop-up mystery. Adhere the finished copies to a mini file folder die cut to finish the look of a detective case file. Begin your search by going to http://www2.scholastic.com/browse/unitplan.jsp?id=241

Other great mystery resources:

♦ *Writing Mysteries in the Classroom* by Cheryl Garrett

♦ "Anatomy of a Mystery" can be found at http://library.thinkquest.org/J002344/Anatomy.html

♦ Quick mysteries to use with students are available at http://kids.mysterynet.com

Memoir: My Life As...

A favorite unit for students and teachers alike is the memoir unit, à la Lucy, where students write about their own life. A favorite text for students to read is *Marley, A Dog Like No Other*, in conjunction with this unit. This *Marley* is the children's version of the bestselling book by John Grogan. Reading the book and discussing how the author writes about his life through the lens of being Marley's owner helps students shape their thinking about the lens they will choose for their writing.

Students should be encouraged to write "chapters," for their own memoir, illustrate them, and then record them. Garage Band is a possible software choice, but any form of audio recording, including the old-fashioned cassette tape recorder (what?) would be acceptable for the purpose of voice recording. Recording it digitally so that it can be exported as an mp3 file works really wells and give lots of options for sharing.

Have your students approach the writing from the focus of what they can teach someone by sharing a glimpse of our life with them. This is very similar to personal essay in that regard; they should be trying to get to big thinking, the "Aha!" thinking. It is key to spend a lot of time talking about themes in literature throughout the year. This helps greatly with writing memoirs.

Memoirs can be typed or handwritten, particularly if you like the handwritten look better. It does look more personal, not so polished. It can be painfully slow to do all that typing also. Whatever works in the grand scheme is the approach to take. The finished book and compact disc set make a really nice end of the year gift for parents. Students feel quite accomplished when they get their memoir completed.

Other Resources Worth Reviewing

It wouldn't be possible to wrapup this book without mentioning with some excellent sites that give access to great resources. Think of the following links as a map for a treasure hunt. Enjoy the adventure; I've tried to point you in good directions while leading you to a point where there is lots to explore.

Let's start with famous quotes. Words mean everything to writers, and who doesn't love a good quote? Share them with students. Sometimes students can write off quotes or use them as a thesis statement for an essay; they can be the caption for an illustration; the options are endless. There are some sites that have really good, famous quotes.

- http://www.brainyquote.com/
- http://www.famous-quotes-and-quotations.com/
- http://koti.mbnet.fi/pasenka/quotes/q-writ.htm#About%20 ideas

Nothing to write about? No way! There are plenty of story starters and journal prompts out there. Here are a few sites to get the writing wheels turning.

- ◆ Writing prompts, more:
  http://www.canteach.ca/elementary/prompts.html
- ◆ Visit the Write on Reader site by going to:
  http://library.thinkquest.org/J001156/writing%20process/
  sl_storystarters.htm

Other miscellaneous stuff, graphic organizers, etc:

- ◆ Can Teach: http://www.canteach.ca/elementary/englangarts.html
- ◆ Ed Helper, graphic organizers and more:
  http://www.edhelper.com/teachers/graphic_organizers.htm
- ◆ Scholastic, graphic organizers galore:
  http://printables.scholastic.com/printables/
  search/?query=graphic%20organizers
- ◆ Write More, check the free activities and resources:
  http://www.writemorestuff.com/pages/activities.html

Putting It All Together

Planning a year of effective, captivating writing instruction can seem like a uphill battle. To help ease the burden, sample overviews of writing units are included in the following figures. Whether teaching for a year, a decade or an entire lifetime, educators must allow themselves the freedom to make writing instruction work for both teacher and student. The following samples can be used as is or adapted.

Figure 7.5. Sample Unit Overview Part 1

Narrative Unit—Part 1

Objective: Students write tight, focusing on a moment in time, creating a small moment narrative piece

Prewriting:

- List special people
- List special places
- List special objects
- Choose one from list and think of a memory connected with it, write a seed
- Generate a number of seeds; choose the best for drafting

Drafting:

- Choose a topic
- Stretch it
- Conventions mini lessons

Revising:

- Revision strategy mini lessons (3–5)
  - Pump up your words (why we revise)
  - Actions
  - Dialogue
  - Thoughts and feelings
  - Descriptive language
- Partner conferences

Edit (do a two-minute edit each day also)

- Editing stations (each station, students use a different color pen)
  - Spelling
  - Punctuation
  - Capitalization
  - Sentence structure
  - Paragraphs

Final Copy/Publish

Celebration: Share with writing buddies from a different grade level

Resource materials: *Every Living Thing* by Cynthia Rylant, other narrative texts

Figure 7.6. Sample Unit Overview Part 2

Narrative Unit—Part 2

Objective: Students hone narrative writing skills, get familiar with writing process and write a personal narrative to be included in a class anthology.

Prewriting:

- Review topic lists: special people, special places, special objects
- Generate lists of strong feelings associated with a memory
- Generate seeds related to strong feelings/emotions (e.g., a time when I felt sad; a time when I felt embarrassed; a time when I felt joyful)

Drafting:

- Choose a topic
- Stretch it
- Conventions mini lessons (as needed)
- Leads
- Endings

Revising:

- Revision strategy mini lessons (3–5)
- Partner conferences

Edit (do a two-minute edit each day also)

- Editing stations (each station, students use a different color pen)
  - Spelling
  - Punctuation
  - Capitalization
  - Sentence structure
  - Paragraphs

Final Copy/Publish: compile a class anthology

Celebration: Share with writing buddies; publish a copy to be housed in school library

Resource materials: picture books reflective of personal narrative genre

Figure 7.7. Sample Unit Assessment

Name _____ Room _____ Date _____

Self-Assessment—Personal Narrative

Title of My Narrative: _____

Is my story a personal narrative? (Does it retell a small moment or a memory from my life? Does it describe a time when…?)

Yes   or   No

An example of how I used descriptive language in my narrative:

_____

_____

	Not at all	Sometimes	Usually	Always
Have I used paragraphs in my final copy?	1	2	3	4
Have I used correct punctuation?	1	2	3	4
Did I use correct spelling or correct my spelling?	1	2	3	4

Revision strategies I used: (give examples)

_____

_____

Some ways I edited my writing: (give examples)

_____

_____

3 Things I did well when I wrote my narrative:

*

*

*

2 Things I need to work harder on in the future:

*

*

1 Thing I would like my teacher to help me with in the future:

*

Figure 7.8. Sample Unit Overview

Fiction Unit Overview
(in conjunction with National Novel
Writing Month/November)

Objective: Students will select a topic from previously generated list of topics, develop a fiction short story and a novel from their personal lists.

Introducing it:

♦ Countdown to NaNo WriMo on door (this generates excitement as students wonder what NaNo WriMo is)

♦ Begin discussing the elements of fiction: characters, setting, plot, etc. Create plot roller coaster and create 3 characters, bringing them to life by giving them names, hobbies, likes, dislikes, etc.

♦ Prep goal-setting materials

♦ Notebooks for novels

Goal setting:

♦ Give a writing prompt; have students write for 8–10 minutes

♦ Count words written

♦ Set a goal—should be attainable; discuss attaining/exceeding goals

♦ Students write each night for 20 nights, trying to achieve their personal word count goal

♦ Each day they record if they achieved (or exceeded) their goal

Progress monitoring:

♦ Individual writing goal charts

  • Assemble

  • Post prominently (bulletin board, desk, or locker)

  • Discuss the importance of honesty and personal goals

  • Students record progress daily

♦ Partner conferences

Final Copy/Publish: (at later time, if desired)

Resource materials: NaNo WriMo website, various examples of novels and short stories

Figure 7.9. Sample Unit Assessment (Page 1)

Name _____ Room _____ Date _____

Self-Assessment: Fiction

Title of My Short Story: _____

The plot roller coaster for my short story: (sketch it here)

	Not at all	Sometimes	Usually	Always
Have I used paragraphs in my final copy?	1	2	3	4
Have I used correct punctuation?	1	2	3	4
Did I use correct spelling or correct my spelling?	1	2	3	4

Revision strategies I used: (give examples)

_____

_____

Some ways I edited my writing: (give examples)

_____

_____

3 Things I did well when I wrote my short story:

*

*

*

2 Things I need to work harder on in the future:

*

*

1 thing I would like my teacher to help me with:

Figure 7.9. Sample Unit Assessment (Page 2)

Title of My Novel: _____

The plot of my novel: _____

_____

_____

_____

_____

_____

Describe the main character in the novel: _____

_____

_____

_____

_____

Who else is in the novel? Describe them: _____

_____

_____

_____

_____

My daily word count goal was:

I achieved my goal _____ out of 20 days. I exceeded my goal _____ out of 20 days.

3 Things I did well when I wrote my novel:

*

*

*

2 Things I need to work harder on in the future:

*

*

Note to Teachers: Copy pages 1 and 2 back to back.

Figure 7.10. Sample Unit Overview

Poetry Unit Overview

Prewriting:

- ◆ What do we know about poetry? (carousel activity using chart paper and small groups)
- ◆ Review idea/topic lists: special people, special places, objects
- ◆ Add any new ideas to those lists
- ◆ Read, study the work of numerous poets in groups of 2–3 students (plan to have 8–10 poetry books per student group).

Drafting: (Over the unit, examine 5–10 styles of poetry, write at least 5 styles)

- ◆ Two-word, line poem
- ◆ Free verse
- ◆ Couplets
- ◆ Rhymed verse
- ◆ Poetry theater (write script with small group 2–3 students)

Revising:

- ◆ Revision strategy mini lessons (3–5)
  - ● Pump up your words (why we revise)
  - ● Action words
  - ● Descriptive language
- ◆ Partner share

Edit (as needed)

Final Copy/Publish

Decorate Poet Tree with individual poems

Finished script

Celebration: Present and record using camcorder

Resource materials: variety of poem, poetry anthologies, thesaurus

Figure 7.11. Sample Unit Assessment

Name _____ Room _____ Date _____

Self-Assessment: Poetry Unit

Title of my Poetry Theater script: _____

Who are the members of your group?

_____

_____

What is the plot of the script?

_____

_____

Is the script written in poetry format   Yes   or   No

An example of how I used descriptive language in my narrative:

_____

_____

How did the props enhance the presentation?

_____

_____

Revision strategies I used: (give examples)

_____

_____

Some ways I edited my writing: (give examples)

_____

_____

3 other forms of poetry I wrote during this unit:

*

*

*

2 things I enjoy about poetry:

*

*

1 thing I would like my teacher to help me with in the future:

*

Figure 7.12. Sample Unit Overview

Personal Essay Unit

Objective: Students will craft personal essays using a "This, I Believe" format (see NPR radio programming).

Prewriting:

- ◆ Review lists: special people, special places, special objects
- ◆ Students generate individual lists of "I believe" statements
- ◆ Choose one "I believe" statement and create a thesis statement based on the "I believe" statement.

Drafting:

- ◆ Introductory paragraph using "I believe" statement, thesis statement and two-three others describing the topic.
- ◆ Three supporting paragraphs (three small moments that support the thesis)
- ◆ Concluding paragraph
- ◆ Does it need a better lead?
- ◆ How is my ending?

Revising:

- ◆ Revision strategy mini lessons (3–5)
  - Review previous strategies
  - Thoughts and feelings
  - Move things around
- ◆ Partner conferences

Edit (do a two-minute edit each day also)

- ◆ Editing stations (each station, students use a different color pen)
  - Spelling
  - Punctuation
  - Capitalization
  - Sentence structure
  - Paragraphs

Final Copy/Publish

Celebration: Share with another class/writing buddies

Resource materials:

Figure 7.13. Sample Unit Assessment

Self-Assessment: Personal Essay

Title of My Essay: _____

My "I Believe" statement: _____

_____

The thesis statement for my essay: _____

_____

_____

Three ideas that support my thesis:

1. _____

2. _____

3. _____

	Not at all	Sometimes	Usually	Always
Have I used paragraphs in my final copy?	1	2	3	4
Have I used correct punctuation?	1	2	3	4
Did I use correct spelling or correct my spelling?	1	2	3	4

Revision strategies I used:

_____

_____

_____

Ways I edited my writing:

_____

_____

3 Things I did well when I wrote my essay:

*

*

*

2 Things I need to work harder on in the future:

*

*

1 Thing I would like my teacher to help me with in the future:

*

Figure 7.14. Sample Unit Overview

Memoir Unit

Objective: Students will craft a memoir based on the lens of "My Life as a …"

Prewriting:

♦ Generate a list of all the relationships in student's lives (e.g., I am a daughter, a sister, a cousin, a pet owner, a writer, a gardener.)

♦ Choose one relationship and create a personal statement based on the relationship. (e.g., My life matters. I am a _____.)

Drafting:

♦ 1–8 chapters

♦ Write through the lens of "My Life as a…"

♦ Great beginnings

♦ Awesome endings

Revising:

♦ Revision strategy mini lessons (3–5)

♦ Partner conferences

Edit (do a two-minute edit each day also)

♦ Editing stations (each station, students use a different color pen)

   ● Spelling

   ● Punctuation

   ● Capitalization

   ● Sentence structure

   ● Paragraphs

Final Copy/Publish: Type final copies on laptops. Record audio using Garage Band. Final product: book/cd set.

Celebration: Share with parents

Resource materials: *Marley, A Dog Like No Other* by John Grogan. (This is the version of *Marley* adapted for students.)

A Last Thought

Once you have implemented some of the ideas and tried them out, give yourself some time to reflect on what you did, whether it was as successful as you thought it would be, and, most importantly, how it could be made better. Of course, every year your class will be different—a different mix of writing strengths and instructional needs. Each year the mix of parents will be different. Some will be willing partners in writing, whereas others will need more encouragement and handholding. Every effort you make will reap rewards in student achievement.

Come back to this book often, revisit the ideas and make adjustments as needed. Always remember to enjoy the successes your students experience each day as they write. A nation of strong writers is being built a page at a time.

References

Adler, Mortimer J. *The Paideia Proposal*. New York: Macmillan, 1982.

Ballenger, Bruce. "Donald Murray and the Pedagogy of Surprise." Available at: http://www.boisestate.edu/english/bballenger/Ballenger_Reconsiderations.pdf. Last accessed: July 23, 2010.

Brainstorm Gallery, The. "Quotes about Writing." http://koti.mbnet.fi/pasenka/quotes/q- main.htm. Last accessed July 22, 2010.

Calkins, Lucy. *Units of Study for Primary Writing: A Yearlong Curriculum*. Portsmouth, NH: Heinemann, 2003.

Calkins, Lucy. *Units of Study for Teaching Writing Grades 3–5*. Portsmouth, NH: Heinemann, 2006.

Fletcher, Ralph. "Handouts for Teachers." Available at: www.ralphfletcher.com/teacher.html. Last accessed: July 22, 2010.

National Commission on Writing, The. "The Neglected R," (2003). Available at www.vantagelearning.com/docs/myaccess/neglectedr.pdf. Last accessed: July 22, 2010.

National Writing Project, The. "Learning to Write, Writing to Learn: Americans' Views of Writing in Our Schools." Available at: http://www.nwp.org/cs/public/download/nwp_file/4532/Americans_Views_of_Writing_in _Our_Schools.pdf?x-r=pcfile_d. Last accessed: July 22, 2010.

Rothman, Donald. "The Writing Revolution." *Santa Cruz Sentinel*. (2003). Available at: http://www.cateweb.org/california_english/ce_2003_september.htm. Last accessed: July 22, 2010.

Sentz, Lynda. *Writing by Heart: The Study of Parents as Writing Role Models and the Impact on Student Writing*. Buffalo: State University College of New York at Buffalo, 2009.

Smith, Frank. *Writing and the Writer*. Hillsdale, NJ: Lawrence Erlbaum Associates, 1994.

Strawser, Jessica. "Thomas Steinbeck: Like Father, Like Son." *Writers Digest*, 2003. Available at: http://www.writersdigest.com/article/thomas-steinbeck/. Last accessed: July 22, 2010.

U.S. Department of Education, Institute of Education Sciences. "The Nation's Report Card: Writing Highlights." National Center for Education Statistics, 2003. Available at: http://nces.ed.gov/nationsreportcard/. Last accessed: Dec. 3, 2005.

U.S. Department of Labor. "Time Spent in Primary Activities," 2008. Available at: http://www.bls.gov/news.release/atus.t08.htm. Last accessed: March 26, 2009.

Vassallo, Philip. "More Than Grades: How Parent Choice Boosts Parental Involvement and Benefits Children." *Policy Analysis*, 383. CATO Institute, (2000). Available at: http://www.cato.org/pubs/pas/pa-383es.html. Last accessed: Feb. 25, 2009.

Wollman-Bonilla, Julie E. *Family Message Journals: Teaching Writing Through Family Involvement.* Urbana, IL: National Council of Teachers of English, 2000.

Yancey, Kathleen Blake. "Writing in the 21st Century." NCTE. Available at: http://www.ncte.org/library/NCTEFiles/Press/Yancey_final.pdf. Last accessed: Dec. 28, 2009.